D0828103

STUDIES FOR NEW CONVERTS

... BY ...

PRICE ROBERTS

STANDARD PUBLISHING
CINCINNATI, OHIO

CONTENTS

KNOW YOUR BIBLE

Bible Drill on the Books of the Bible

1. Question: What is the greatest Book in the world?
Answer: The Bible.

2. Q. Give two names for the Bible found within it.

A. Word of God and the Scriptures.

3. Q. Into what two great divisions has the Bible been divided?

A. The Old and the New Testaments.

4. Q. How many books are there in the Old Testament?

A. Thirty-nine.

5. Q. How many books are there in the New Testament?

A. Twenty-seven.

6. Q. Into what five groups may the books of the Old Testament be divided?

A. Law, history, devotions, major prophets and minor prophets.

7. Q. How many books are there of law?

A. Five.

8. Q. Name them.

A. Gen'-e-sis, Ex'-o-dus, Le-vit'-i-cus, Numbers and Deu-ter-on'-o-my.

9. Q. How many books are there of history?

A. Twelve.

10. Q. Name them.

A. Josh'-u-a, Judges, Ruth, 1 Samuel, 2 Samuel, 1 Kings, 2 Kings, 1 Chronicles, 2 Chronicles, Ezra, Ne-he-mi'-ah and Esther.

11. Q. How many books are there of devotions?

A. Five.

12. Q. Name them.

A. Job, Psalms, Proverbs, Ec-cle-si-as'-tes, Song of Sol'-o-mon.

13. Q. How many books are there of the major prophets?

A. Five.

14. Q. Name them.

A. I-sa'-iah, Jer-e-mi'-ah, La-men-ta'-tions, E-ze'-ki-el and Daniel.

15. Q. How many books are there of the minor prophets?

A. Twelve.

16. Q. Name them.

A. Ho-se'-a, Jo'-el, A'-mos, O-ba-di'-ah, Jo'-nah, Mi'-cah, Na'-hum, Ha-bak'-kuk, Zeph-a-ni'-ah, Hag'-gai, Zech-a-ri'-ah and Mal'-a-chi.

17. Q. Into what five groups may the books of the New Testament be divided?

A. Biography, history, special letters, general letters and prophecy.

18. Q. How many books are there of biography?

A. Four.

19. Q. Name them.

A. Matthew, Mark, Luke and John.

20. Q. How many books are there of history?

A. Only one.

21. Q. Name it.

A. The Book of Acts.

22. Q. How many books of special letters are there?

A. Fourteen.

23. Q. Name them.

A. Romans, 1 Co-rin'-thi-ans, 2 Co-rin'-thi-ans, Ga-la'-tians,

E-phe'-sians, Phi-lip -pians, Co-los'-si-ans, 1 Thes-sa-lo'-ni-ans, 2 Thes-sa-lo'-ni-ans, 1 Timothy, 2 Timothy, Ti'-tus, Phi-le'-mon and Hebrews.

24. Q. How many books are there of general letters?

A. Seven.

25. Q. Name them.

A. James, 1 Peter, 2 Peter, 1 John, 2 John, 3 John and Jude.

26. Q. How many books are there of prophecy?

A. Only one.

27. Q. Name it.

A. Revelation.

28. Q. How many books are there in the entire Bible?

A. Sixty-six.

29. Q. Name them.

A. Genesis, Exodus, Leviticus, Numbers, Deuteronomy, Joshua, Judges, Ruth, 1 Samuel, 2 Samuel, 1 Kings, 2 Kings, 1 Chronicles, 2 Chronicles, Ezra, Nehemiah, Esther, Job, Psalms, Proverbs, Ecclesiastes, Song of Solomon, Isaiah, Jeremiah, Lamentations, Ezekiel, Daniel, Hosea, Joel, Amos, Obadiah, Jonah, Micah, Nahum, Habakkuk, Zephaniah, Haggai, Zechariah, Malachi, Matthew, Mark, Luke, John, Acts, Romans, 1 Corinthians, 2 Corinthians, Galatians, Ephesians, Philippians, Colossians, 1 Thessalonians, 2 Thessalonians, 1 Timothy, 2 Timothy, Titus, Philemon, Hebrews, James, 1 Peter, 2 Peter, 1 John, 2 John, 3 John, Jude and Revelation.

Bible Drill on Finding Passages

A. Have pupils stand in a line so that the teacher may walk behind them. When a reference is called, the head of the class and the one next to him compete in finding the verse. The one who finds it first puts his finger on the place and calls "I." The teacher quickly verifies the reference. Proceed as an old-fashioned "spelling bee."

B. The following references are taken one each from every book in the Bible, and are so arranged as to require much searching of the Scriptures. The list may be used for the purpose of having the references read aloud, or merely pointed out according to the directions above. This list may also be used several times over by merely starting at different points in the list and going backward or forward.

Gen. 3 : 15	Tit. 3 : 5	Obad. 4
2 Thess. 1 : 12	Eph. 4 : 4	Josh. 23 : 6
Phile. 3	Ruth 1 : 16, 17	3 John 11
Num. 21 : 9	Mic. 4 : 2	1 Sam. 17 : 50
Ps. 107 : 21	Jas. 1 : 27	1 Pet. 3 : 21
Deut. 29 : 29 .	Jer. 31 : 31	Esth. 4 : 16
Hos. 6 : 6	Eccl. 8 : 5	1 Chron. 17 : 7, 8
1 John 3 : 14	Heb. 2 : 10	1 Cor. 3 : 11
Acts 11 : 26	John 3 : 5	2 Chron. 7 : 14
Mal. 3 : 10	Dan. 2 : 44	Jonah 1 : 15
Ex. 14 : 31	Joel 3 : 13	Hab. 2 : 12
Zech. 7 : 9	Isa. 62 : 2	Zeph. 3 : 13
S. of Sol. 3 : 2	Prov. 4 : 23	Col. 2 : 14
Neh. 4 : 6	Job 38 : 4	Rev. 22 : 18, 19
Judg. 6 : 14	Luke 2 : 52	2 Kings 22 : 2
Lam. 5 : 19	Ezek. 34 : 11	1 Tim. 4 : 12
Amos 5 : 4	Mark 8 : 35	1 Kings 18 : 39
Hag. 2 : 6	1 Thess. 5 : 21	Phil. 3 : 13
2 Cor. 12 : 9	Lev. 19 : 4	2 Pet. 3 : 18
2 Tim. 4 : 1, 2	2 Sam. 12 : 13	2 John 9
Jude 3	Rom. 10 : 10	Gal. 3 : 27
Ez. 7 : 10	Nah. 1 : 15	Matt. 6 : 33

NOTE.—The Bible-drill work in this lesson may seem to be a heavy assignment for one lesson, but it may be split up into as many lessons as the teacher deems advisable.

HOW TO READ THE BIBLE

I. The Bible Is the Most Wonderful Book in the World.

A. *It reveals the most wonderful Person in the world.*

1. Jesus and His coming kingdom are the subjects of the verbal prophecies of the Old Testament. A long list of these prophetic utterances, some of them clear and distinct, and others somewhat obscure, may be discovered as we read carefully the pages of the Old Testament.

2. Besides these there are many types and shadows given in the ordinances, forms and furnishings of the patriarchal and Jewish worship. Among these are the altar of both the patriarchal and Jewish dispensations, the tabernacle and temple of the Jewish dispensation and the various furnishings of these institutions. Everything that had to do with their worship seemed to point forward to some significant event or condition under a future dispensation.

3. There are also some very striking analogies of Christ in some of the characters of the Old Testament, such as Joseph, Moses, Abraham and David, who are sometimes said to be types of Christ.

4. The New Testament is filled with the story of this wonderful Christ. The first four books deal with His life, ministry, death, resurrection and ascension; the Book of Acts reveals His kingdom set up and in action; the Epistles point constantly to Him and His principles of life, and the Book of

Revelation gives a vivid picture of His glorious and triumphant return.

Jesus declared that the Scriptures of the Old Testament testified of Him (John 5:39); John, the writer of the fourth Gospel, says that his record was written that men might believe that He was the Christ, the Son of God (John 20:30, 31); and Paul declared that the Scriptures were given "for teaching, for reproof, for correction, for instruction which is in righteousness" (2 Tim. 3:16).

B. *It reveals the way of salvation through Christ.* The Scriptures are not only able to make us wise, but to "make . . . wise unto salvation" (2 Tim. 3:15).

1. The four Gospels—Matthew, Mark, Luke and John—picture for us a "Saviour who is Christ the Lord." One can scarcely read any one of these Gospel stories and not be convinced that Jesus is "the Christ, the Son of the living God."

2. The Book of Acts tells us of the church the apostles, chosen and trained by Jesus and endowed with the Holy Spirit, had set up. It tells us how men and women were converted and added to the church in the days of the apostles. There are at least eight cases of conversion recorded in this book, and by reading them we may easily discover what men then did to be saved, and what they did then to be saved is a safe guide for us today in the same matter.

3. The New Testament also contains twenty-one Epistles, or letters, written to individuals and churches that constitute a safe guide for us in the matter of the conduct of our lives. They present problems, experience and admonitions covering every phase of life and show us how to meet the conditions of life in every age.

Thus the Bible may be said to be a sharp, two-edged sword, dividing between right and wrong, and discerning to the very depths of our thinking (Heb. 4:12). It constitutes a mirror to the soul so that we may carefully examine

Page 10

ourselves at all times in the light of its teachings (Jas. 1: 21-25).

C. *The Bible not only acquaints us with the Christ as the Son of God and points the way of salvation through Him, but it places a means in our hands by which we may win others to Christ.*

1. The Word of God is the sword of the Spirit (Eph. 6:17) by which we may sever men from their sins. No man can unite with Christ until he is separated from sin.

2. Men are to be saved by the preaching of the Word, however foolish that may seem to men (1 Cor. 1:21; Rom. 10:14; 2 Tim. 4:1-12).

3. His Word will not return unto Him void (Isa. 55:11). Every Christian should study the Word of God that he may be able to use this "sword of the Spirit" in winning others to Christ. One does not need to know many other things, or to be a fluent speaker, but he should be familiar with the Word if his work is to be effective.

II. Read Your Bible Intelligently.

A. *The Bible, to be understood, should be read and studied like any piece of good literature.*

1. The best literature must not only be read, but studied, to be fully appreciated. One can not read Milton or Shakespeare like a popular novel or an easy-flowing rime. Works like this contain depths of meaning that must be mined by careful thinking.

2. The Bible must be studied. The one who expects to grasp its great messages by carelessly running over the words will be disappointed, but the one who will take the pains to search for hidden meanings will find a wealth and beauty continually new. Paul admonishes Timothy, a young evangelist, to "study" the Scriptures, and he gave him three reasons for such study: That he might be approved of God,

a workman unashamed and able to handle aright the Word (2 Tim. 2:15). Why should any one attempt to teach a Bible-school class, or in any way teach the Bible, who has made no study of his subject? We do not attempt to teach any other subject without preparation. Is the Bible, which contains the message of eternal life, of less importance than other subjects?

3. By a careful study and knowledge of the Scriptures we will be able to weigh and judge the teachings of those who preach or instruct us. The people of Berea received Paul's gospel readily, because they were daily searching the Scriptures to see if these things were so (Acts 17:11). They did not merely glance at them, but they "searched" them. One may be easily led into all kinds of false teachings who fails to study the Bible.

B. *The Bible, to be read intelligently, must be read constantly.*

1. The one who picks up his Bible for a few minutes on Sunday morning only, and expects to appreciate its message, is only wasting time. It is only the one who reads it regularly and continually who will be initiated into the light and beauty it reveals. If you will read again Acts 17:11, you will discover that the Bereans not only searched the Scriptures, but they searched them "daily."

2. One should have a set time for Bible study and allow nothing to interfere with that time. It is not so much the amount of time you spend upon it as it is the regularity of your study that counts. It would be better to spend one hour a day for seven days than to spend seven hours in one day in Bible study and then rest for a whole week. We can not give all our time to Bible study in this busy world in which we live, but most people could set apart a definite time each day if they would but make the effort.

C. *In any careful study of the Bible the following "rule of three" will be of value:*

1. Know who is speaking. Although everything in the Bible was recorded under the inspiration of the Holy Spirit, not every saying in the Bible comes from inspired men. (a) The Bible records the sayings of very much misguided men. As an illustration read Mark 9:5, 6. Here Peter speaks out of turn and seeks to advise the Lord what should be done. His statement is recorded, but he certainly was not speaking by the Spirit of God, therefore his statement is not authoritative. Similar statements of misguided men recorded in the Scriptures might be multiplied if we had the room here. (b) The Bible also records the sayings of evil-minded men. The scribes and Pharisees who crucified the Saviour had much to say as He hung upon the cross. Their statements were many times not even true, and yet the Bible contains a record of them. Read Matt. 27:38-45. (c) Even the statements of demons, whether true or false, are recorded in the Bible (Matt. 4:1-11). Thus it becomes apparent that if we are to read the Bible intelligently, we must know who is speaking.

2. Know who is being addressed. Ask yourself such questions as these: Does the passage I am reading apply to this dispensation or age, or a former one? Does it apply to Christians or sinners? Is the speaker addressing some one, or meditating in his own heart? We can not possibly understand the Scriptures unless we know who is speaking and who is being addressed, and we can not know these things without reading more than a verse or two. The trouble with too much of our reading is that we do not partake of the Bible in sufficient amounts, but read too often a few scattered verses that really carry no definite meaning to our hearts.

3. It is also well, in reading any book of the Bible, to ascertain and keep in mind the purpose for which the book was written. Matthew was written for the Jews, or rather from the Jewish viewpoint; Mark was written for the Romans; Luke was written for the Greeks; John was written for the church in general; Acts is a partial history of the church

during its beginning and early development; Paul wrote to various churches to correct their evils, encourage and unify them and induce them to greater endeavor. There is a purpose for every book of the Bible, and it will be well for us to remember that purpose as we read.

D. *Good Bible helps are a great aid in the study of the Bible.*

1. A systematic course of study is the best plan if we can find time for it. There are many good courses on the market, but care should be exercised in selection. Generally the best plan would be to master those courses which are being given in your Bible school, or to ask the advice of some preacher or good Bible student before you make your selection.

2. A good Bible is a first essential. It should have at least a brief introduction to each book and a good cross-reference system. Other features may be included, but the two we mention are almost indispensable to a careful and understanding study.

3. Every Bible student should have a complete concordance and learn how to use it. It helps to find more readily desired passages and makes one more familiar with the subject matter of the Bible.

These are by no means all the helps that may be used to advantage, but they do constitute a very good set of working tools for Bible study.

III. Read Your Bible Prayerfully.

A. *It is the Word of God and should be approached reverently.*

1. No literature is worthy to be compared with it in this respect. It is not the words of men, but the Word of God. It is Jehovah's dealings with men that constitutes its subject matter, and the Spirit of God hovered near and watched over it as it was being penned. It was preserved for our

reading by the power of this same Spirit, and comes down to us today as a rich legacy from on high. Let us handle it with care. Let us approach it with reverence and godly fear.

B. *Constant meditation upon the Word brings strength and blessing.*

1. The "hurry up and get it done" kind of reading can not be profitable. We must come to sit down quietly to receive God's message for us. We must have our minds free from other things that the Word may "have free course and run and be glorified" in our lives.

2. This meditation should not be spasmodic, but constant. An occasional meal would not be very healthful to our physical bodies. Neither will an occasional reading of God's Word feed the soul. We need this Word constantly to feed and fill our minds and hearts, so that in every emergency, in every sorrow and at the approach of each new task we may have the Bible as our guide and chart of life.

C. *A prayerful study of the Bible will make us fit to have a place in life.*

1. Great men have been readers of the Bible and it has influenced their thinking and their lives greatly. We have not space here for extended statements or a long list of names, but we mention a few who have been greatly influenced by the reading of the Bible: William Gladstone, Benjamin Franklin, George Washington, Thomas Jefferson, Abraham Lincoln, William McKinley, Woodrow Wilson and Theodore Roosevelt are among the greatest of our statesmen, and the Bible has had a telling influence upon their lives. Edmund Burke, Elizabeth Fry, Lord Shaftesbury, William Wilberforce and William Lloyd Garrison are some of the world's greatest reformers, and their lives were first touched and ennobled by a constant reading of the Word of God. Many others among the characters of history could be mentioned testifying to the power of the Bible in shaping their lives and making them truly great. Is it not worth while for us to allow the

Bible to help us to develop a great, noble and worth-while character?

2. The Psalmist says that the man who meditates upon the Word will be like a tree planted by the rivers of waters (Ps. 1:1-6). He describes a man who not only reads the Bible, but who "meditates" upon it constantly—"day and night." He is always green and growing, and brings forth fruit in proper season. Whatever he does prospers, because it is built upon a secure foundation. On the other hand, the man who does not meditate upon the Word, but spends his time with the ungodly, will wither and die, because he has starved his soul when there was bread enough and to spare.

Let us accept this Bible as the most wonderful book in the world; as "the word of God, which liveth and abideth for ever." Let us read it intelligently and prayerfully, that its teachings may beautify, strengthen and bless our lives.

A NEW LIFE IN CHRIST

I. As Christians We Have Had a New Birth.

A. *We have been begotten through the Word of God.*

1. The Word of God is a spiritual seed sown in the heart (Matt. 13:18-23). We are not born into the kingdom by any instantaneous experience, but by a gradual process of the development of spiritual seed. In describing the kingdom in this passage, Jesus speaks of the Word as passing through a variety of experiences in different soils which involved the element of time: (a) It died out for lack of proper rooting (vs. 20, 21); (b) it was choked out by the cares of this world and the deceitfulness of riches (v. 22); (c) it fell upon good soil and brought forth fruit (v. 23). The Word does not die out instantly, but gradually, like a plant. Neither the Word nor a seed is choked out in a flash, but is gradually choked out by other plants. The bearing and bringing forth of fruit is not a momentary process, but one that takes weeks and sometimes months. Just so the Word of God, which is a spiritual seed when planted in the heart, dies out slowly, if it dies out; or, if it does not die, it develops slowly, like a plant.

2. We are born of a seed, which is the Word of God (1 Pet. 1:23). A seed does not burst full grown into a plant, but must develop and grow before it creeps forth from its prison house of earth. Just so the seed of the kingdom, which is the

Word of God when planted in the human mind, must germinate and grow before it can come forth into the light of a new day as a new creature in Christ.

3. In the record of the conversions in the Book of Acts there is invariably an indication that the Word of God was first planted in the heart by the preaching of the gospel. (a) On the day of Pentecost the apostles preached the Word of God before there were any conversions (Acts 2: 14-41) ; (b) at Samaria, Philip's preaching was heard and believed before there were any baptisms (Acts 8: 5-8, 12) ; (c) to the Ethiopian eunuch Philip "preached unto him Jesus" before he decided to be baptized (Acts 8: 26-40) ; (d) Saul of Tarsus heard the impassioned preaching of the martyr Stephen before he was converted (Acts 7: 54-60) ; (e) Peter preached to the house of Cornelius before the coming of the Holy Spirit and their baptism (Acts 10: 34-48) ; (f) Lydia of Philippi "attended unto the things spoken by Paul" before she was baptized (Acts 16: 14, 15) ; (g) and Paul "spake the word of the Lord" to the Philippian jailer and to all that were in his house (Acts 16: 23-34). In all the recorded cases of conversion in the New Testament, the Word, sown in the heart, brought forth newborn children of God.

4. The Word, sown in the heart, produces a child of God according to a divine plan. Its first work is to produce faith out of which grows all the other elements of conversion. "Faith comes by hearing . . . the word of God" (Rom. 10: 17). Faith comes by hearing the testimony of competent witnesses as to the deity of Jesus. Having accepted such testimony, we are brought to see a crucified and risen Lord, which, seeing in turn, produces repentance in the heart. It is "the goodness of God" that leads men to repentance (Rom. 2: 4). When one has thus believed on this Christ of the Scriptures, or Word of God, and been enabled through this same Word of God to see this wonderful Christ bleeding and dying for his sins, "godly sorrow," which brings forth re-
Page 18

pentance, is produced in the heart (2 Cor. 7:9, 10). When one sees this same Christ risen from the dead with power and authority, he is both willing and anxious to surrender his life to Him and acknowledge Him as his King before men. Thus he is brought to the place of an open confession of Christ before men according to Christ's command (Matt. 10:32, 33). The cumulative results of this expanding seed, the Word of God planted in the heart, bring one naturally to the place of complete and willing obedience to God, and he is then gladly immersed and becomes a newborn child of God.

B. *We have been born of water and Spirit together.*

1. John 3:5-8 does not teach that one must have two births, one of the water and another of the Spirit. Nor does it teach that one must have a birth of the Spirit alone. It teaches rather that there are two agents active in the process of regeneration, just as there are two agents in the natural birth, or first generation. As there must be father and mother in the physical birth, so there must be Spirit and water in the spiritual birth. The word *Spirit* in all English translations is masculine gender, and the word *water,* in the Latin at least, is feminine. Thus it would seem that we are begotten by the Spirit and born of the water.

2. As immersion is the only act practiced for baptism which can be said to describe a birth, we may safely conclude that immersion, not sprinkling or pouring, is that which the Lord commanded and had in mind in John 3:5-8.

II. Having Been Born Again, We Have Changed Our Condition, Relationship and State in Life.

A. *We have been saved from a lost to a saved condition.*

1. There are numerous passages of Scripture that indicate that man, without divine intervention, is lost: (a) In three great parables Jesus pictures man as lost and the angels of God rejoicing when he is found and returned (Luke 15:3-32);

(b) Jesus sent out His disciples to "the lost sheep of the house of Israel" (Matt. 15:24). Paul said, "Our gospel is hid to them that are lost" (2 Cor. 4:3). Many other passages could be added proving the same point.

2. There are other passages that show that since one is in Christ he is saved: (a) Jesus said, "He that believeth and is baptized shall be saved" (Mark 16:15, 16); (b) on the day of Pentecost the "Lord added to them such as were saved" (Acts 2:47); (c) Paul declared that "according to his mercy he saved us" (Tit. 3:5). Other passages could be added to this list.

B. *Our relationship has been changed from that of an alien to a child of God.*

1. At one time we were all alienated, or made strangers to God (Col. 1:20, 21). We have no moral right to charge this alienated relationship to Adam, for we are ourselves individually responsible for it. Through our own personal sins we have turned our backs upon God and have thus become aliens, or strangers to God. In his prophecy concerning the new dispensation, Isaiah says, "All we like sheep have gone astray" (Isa. 53:6).

2. But we who are Christians, who have been born again, have been reconciled to God through the sacrifice of His Son (Rom. 5:8-11; 2 Cor. 5:17-21; Col. 1:19-22; Heb. 2:17).

3. We have been changed from the relationship of strangers to that of fellow citizens of the household of faith: (a) Israel was God's only people before the coming of Christ. They were the recipients of His especial favors and the custodians of all things sacred under the law (Acts 7:37, 38; Rom. 3:1, 2; 4). (b) While they constituted the household of God, it was not a household of faith. It was rather a household of law, and all Gentiles were strangers to it (Eph. 2:12). (c) Christ both fulfilled and abolished the law in His crucifixion (Matt. 5:17; Col. 2:14), and made *faith* rather than *law* the basis of the new covenant (Eph. 2:8). (d) The

Page 20

Jews, who were servants in bondage under the law, became sons by adoption into the household of faith (Gal. 4:1-7). (e) Under this new and better way the Gentiles who were afar off were "made nigh by the blood of Christ" (Eph. 2:11-13). (f) Thus both Jews and Gentiles were brought into the same household, the household of faith. The middle wall of partition has been broken down, the law has been abolished, and in Christ both Jews and Gentiles have become one body. We are, therefore, "no more strangers and foreigners, but fellow-citizens with the saints and of the household of God" (Eph. 2:19).

C. *We have been changed from a dead to a living state in Christ.*

1. No matter how well the Jew lived up to the law, he was nevertheless dead without Christ. The law was "the ministration of death" (2 Cor. 3:7-9). Without Christ they were still under the condemnation of death pronounced, because of Adam's transgression, upon all who sin (1 Cor. 15: 22). That is a false doctrine which teaches that Adam's sin is imputed to all men in all ages. Adam's sin was never imputed to any one but Adam. "By one man [Adam] sin entered into the world, and death by sin, and so death passed upon all." That is, Adam's sin was the occasion of the first pronouncement of the sentence of death for sin. The penalty of death for sin existed before this pronouncement, but Adam's sin was the occasion of its pronouncement. This penalty pronounced upon Adam for his sin must of necessity apply to all men, for it was, and is, a fundamental law of God, so that all men who sin will fall under the same condemnation. Notice that "death passed upon all," not because Adam had sinned, but because "all sinned" (Rom. 5:12). The Jew was under this condemnation, even though he belonged to the household of God, and, as soon as he came to the age of accountability and sinned, the sentence of spiritual death, already pronounced, applied to him. There was, however, a provision

for the righteous Jew, so that in the sacrifice of Christ he might be made alive (Heb. 10:1-14).

2. All Jews and Gentiles living in the Christian dispensation may be saved by the same provisions of faith in Christ (Rom. 3:28-30). As Christians now—neither Jew nor Gentile —we "have passed from death unto life" (John 5:24). "The law of the Spirit of life in Christ Jesus hath made us free from the law of sin and death" (Rom. 8:2).

III. In This New Life in Christ We Must Separate Ourselves from the World.

The world belongs to Satan and is in many ways directly contrary to the will of Christ. To hold onto the world is to lose Christ; to hold onto Christ is to lose the world. "Ye cannot serve God and mammon."

A. *We must be willing, if need be, to forsake all for Christ.* He requires a full surrender of our lives to Him, and anything short of this disqualifies us as His disciples.

1. The rich young ruler failed because he would not make this full surrender (Mark 10:17-22). He had kept the law to the letter, and, in so doing, surrendered many of the comforts and pleasures of life; but when the Lord asked him to surrender the one thing most dear to himself—namely, his money—he "went away sorrowing," because he was unwilling to give it up.

2. There can be no middle ground in the matter of our surrender to the Lord. We are either free from sin and the servants of Christ, or free from Christ and the servants of sin. We are either working with Christ or we are working against Him (Matt. 12:30).

3. We must lay aside every weight and master every weakness in the race which we are to run (Heb. 12:1, 2). Sometimes the pleasures and desires of the flesh outweigh, in our poor scales, the blessings of an eternal life with God; some-

times some particular habit of ours is the sin to which we fall an easy prey, but we must sacrifice the pleasures of this life, if need be, and overcome our sinful habits and inclinations, making a complete surrender to the will of Christ.

4. We must not allow the affairs of this present life to engross us too deeply (2 Tim. 2:4). Many who have become new creatures in Christ are overcome by worldly interests and eventually lost.

5. Our surrender to Christ must be so complete that we will be ready to forsake all, even to our best friends and our loved ones, if need be, for our blessed Lord (Matt. 10:37).

B. *We must present a holy life unto God.*

1. Under the Jewish dispensation, the animals offered upon the altar had to be without spot or blemish (Lev. 22:20). Under Christ our lives must be as nearly perfect as possible.

2. We must not only come to Him with a cleansed heart at the time we become children of God, but we must continue to live holy lives (Heb. 12:14).

C. *We must separate ourselves from the world.*

1. We should not exclude ourselves from the world, but refrain from practicing the sins of the world (John 17:14, 15). Christians are not of the world, even though they live in the world. We must make contacts with men if we are to save them. We are "the light of the world" and "the salt of the earth," and the lighting and leavening power of our lives is God's means of drawing men unto Himself. But while we have fellowship with men and women of the world in many ways, we must not have fellowship with, or any part in, their unrighteousness (2 Cor. 6:14-18).

He who would be a friend of the world is the enemy of God (Jas. 4:4). Thus we go back to our opening statement and say that the world and Christ can not be reconciled because the world belongs to Satan. Satan is the prince of this world (John 12:31; 14:30; 16:11). Jesus is the Prince of life (Acts 3:15; 5:31; Rev. 1:5). You and I dare not join forces with Satan, but with all our hearts we must serve the Christ. Thus the new life, hid with Christ in God, will grow and flourish, becoming more nearly perfect and more beautiful each day, bearing rich fruitage while we remain upon the earth, and making a rich reward for us, when we shall come into our eternal inheritance.

CHURCH ATTENDANCE

I. The Church Is a Divine Provision for Man's Ultimate Salvation (Matt. 16: 18).

A. *It is the result of divine selection.*

1. Of all the means at His disposal which He might have used in saving men, Jesus selected the church as His chief agency. He might have organized a great political state over which He would have been head: (a) The devil suggested just such a course in the temptation in the wilderness (Matt. 4: 8, 9). (b) After the feeding of the five thousand the multitudes "would have taken him by force and made him king" over just such a kingdom (John 6: 1-15). (c) The apostles thought of Him as an earthly king even after His resurrection and just before His ascension (Acts 1: 6). But Jesus steadfastly refused every suggestion and proposal of an earthly kingdom or any kind of an organized state, and declared that He would build His church against which the gates of hell should not prevail.

2. Men today in their wisdom, or lack of it, ignore the wise provisions of the Infinite and conceive and devise schemes of their own for man's moral and spiritual life and growth, but there can be no successful rival and no adequate substitute for that which the Lord has given us in the church of the living God. For the very foolishness of God is wiser than the wisdom of men (1 Cor. 1: 25).

B. *The church is divine in its content.*

1. It is built upon a divine foundation. Jesus said, "Upon this *rock* I will build my church." Paul declared that Christ was the chief corner stone in the foundation of the apostles and prophets (Eph. 2:20), and that "other foundation can no man lay than that which is laid, which is Jesus Christ" (1 Cor. 3:11).

2. It has a divine head in the person of Christ (Eph. 1:22; 5:23). To Him has been given all authority (Matt. 28:18) and the pre-eminence in all things (Col. 1:18).

3 It has a divine name. It is not an accident that the church has been named for Christ, but a part of the plan of infinite wisdom. It was prophesied long years before the church came into being (Isa. 62:2; 65:15), and it is God's plan to name the whole family, both in heaven and on earth, for Him (Eph. 3:14, 15).

4. It has a divine creed. Not a series of statements of beliefs which are generally thought of as creeds, but a divine object of faith in the person of Jesus Christ as expressed in Peter's confession (Matt. 16:16). All else in the Christian system centers in Christ and revolves about the personality of Christ.

C. *It is divine in its life.*

1. It is the body of Christ (Eph. 5:30; Col. 1:24). It is true that the church has its human element and content, since it is composed of human beings, but the provisions for man's salvation are divine and will admit of no tampering or changing by man.

2. It has a divine guide in the person of the Holy Spirit (John 16:13). It was the Holy Spirit that guided the apostles as they proclaimed the conditions of salvation (Acts 2:1-21), that directed the activities of the first evangelists (Acts 8:26; 10:1-16, 19, 20; 16:6-10), and that inspired the writing of the records that are preserved today (2 Tim. 3: 16, 17).

Page 26

3. It has divine conditions of admission: (a) Faith in Christ as the Son of God (Acts 16:31); (b) repentance towards God for sin (Acts 2:38); (c) a confession of Christ as the Son of God before men (Matt. 10:32, 33), and (d) obedience to the Lord in the immersion of the whole body in water (Acts 8: 26-40).

4. It has divine ordinances: (a) The Lord's Supper was ordained by the Lord (Matt. 26:26-30). (b) Immersion is a divine and not a human ordinance (Matt. 28:18-20).

5. It has a divine message (2 Tim. 3:16, 17; 4:1, 2).

D. *The church is divine in its ownership.*

1. Jesus said the church would be His church (Matt. 16:18).

2. Jesus thought the church of sufficient importance to give His life for it. He loved the church, gave Himself up for it, purchased it with His own precious blood (Eph. 5:25; Acts 20:28). It therefore belongs to Him.

3. The church stands in the same relationship to Christ that the bride does to the bridegroom, or the wife to the husband. (Read John 3:29; Eph. 5:22-32; Rom. 7:2-4.)

4. Christ is coming some day to claim the church as His bride.

(a) Because of this the church must be cleansed for that great day (Eph. 5:26). This cleansing is now going on.

(b) In preparation for this event also the church will be transformed into an incorruptible state (1 Cor. 15:51-58).

(c) In its incorruptible state it will descend from God out of heaven (Rev. 21:2).

(d) Finally the marriage supper of the bride and the Lamb will occur (Rev. 19:6-9), and thus will be consummated the great purpose and plan of God in the church. The gospel will have been preached to the whole world (Matt. 24:14). Its work of evangelizing and edifying having been accomplished, the Lord will claim it as His own (Eph. 5:27).

II. Few People Today Are Conscious of the Importance of Church Attendance.

A. *We have been very zealous in winning souls to Christ through various types of evangelism,* but we have not given very much attention to the equally important matter of holding and developing the spiritual lives of those thus won.

1. We have obeyed the first part of the Great Commission which pertains to evangelism, but we have left almost unnoticed the second part which has to do with the edification and training in Christian service. We are not only to "Go . . . into all the world and preach the gospel to every creature" (Mark 16: 15, 16), but we are also commanded to teach them "to observe all things" He has "commanded" us (Matt. 28: 20).

2. We have brought in great multitudes in revival meetings, and then somehow these babes in Christ have been turned loose among the wolves of the world to shift for themselves, instead of being safely sheltered and protected in the church. The results are that by far the greater per cent of the people whose names are on church books are inactive, nonattendant and in many cases living in sin.

3. We have urged Bible-school attendance and said little or nothing about church attendance, with the result that hundreds attend Bible school each Lord's Day who carelessly turn their backs upon the preaching of the Word, the prayers and the Lord's Table, and walk out. The Bible school is important as a teaching agency in the church, but it should ever remain a servant of the church.

B. *The church has a twofold work.*

1. It affords a means of preaching the gospel, which is the power of God in saving men (Acts 1: 8; Rom. 1: 16). The evangelistic program of the church is of great importance, and without it the church would soon die, but this program is dependent upon the church for its life and power. (a) The church must furnish the men who go out as preachers and

Page 28

evangelists at home and abroad. (b) The church must also furnish the means by which they are sent and kept in the field. (c) The degree of efficiency by which this is done is in proportion to the life and power of the local congregations which send and support them; they constitute the base of supplies for the armies of the Lord.

2. The church is also a means of Christian edification and growth. The church, or household of God, is a building planned or framed by the infinite wisdom of God that grows into a holy temple in the Lord (Eph. 2:19-22). It is in the regular services of the church that our souls are fed and made to grow, and without this growth the results of all our evangelistic efforts would be in vain.

3. If the church is to exert its greatest power, we must observe this twofold program of work. To diligently prosecute the one and leave the other undone is to build a lopsided program that is sadly lacking in efficiency. Jesus not only said, "Go . . . disciple the nations," but He also said, "Feed my sheep," and to leave either of these undone is to fail in our obedience to the Lord and destroy the power and usefulness of the church.

C. *If we are to have a church, we must have church attendance.*

1. While numbers should by no means be the primary objective of the church, it is nevertheless true that numbers add considerably to interest and efficiency of the church. Where two or three are gathered together Christ has promised to be in their midst, but where more are gathered together there is more enthusiasm and power.

2. Christians should, as far as possible, attend every service of the church. Every Christian needs this means of edification and growth which God has provided in the church. We have far too many underfed and undernourished church members who are a total loss to the church and who are fast losing their own souls in the thorn-infested soil of a sinful world.

III. Meeting Together as a Christian Assembly Is God's Means of Edification.

A. *The apostolic church set the example of meeting together.*

1. Jesus had trained the twelve by keeping them together during His earthly ministry, and it is with little wonder that we find them together on the morning of the resurrection (Luke 24: 1-12, 33-35).

2. A week later they are again together when Jesus appears in their midst (John 20: 19-26).

3. When the day of Pentecost came, the 120, including th apostles, were continuing in assembling together in a great protracted meeting (Acts 1: 12—2: 1).

4. After the day of Pentecost they continued this practice of meeting together each Lord's Day (Acts 2: 42).

5. Some years later we find them at Troas, meeting together on the first day of the week (Acts 20: 7).

6. In his letter to the Corinthians, Paul indicated that this meeting together on the first day of the week was a general practice, if not an invariable rule, among the church for which he had ministered in that day (1 Cor. 16: 1, 2). He not only gave orders to the church at Corinth concerning their offerings on that day, but said he had given the same orders to the churches of Galatia. As there were a number of churches in the province of Galatia, we are sure it was the practice of each of them to meet on the first day of the week.

B. *The Christian assembly, or church, had a fourfold program of worship* which was sufficient for man's spiritual needs (Acts 2: 42).

1. It was *educational.* They continued in "the apostle's teaching." Man's spiritual needs include more and more teaching. Christians are born into the kingdom without a full knowledge of the will of Christ. They must grow in knowledge as well as in grace. If this teaching is confined to that which was taught by the apostles, the growth for the

Page 30

individual will be a gradual growth in the understanding of the whole plan of salvation.

2. It was *inspirational*, calling for fellowship in the work and worship of the church. They had fellowship in the teaching, in the offerings, in the prayers, in the singing and in the Lord's Supper.

3. It was a *memorial*, reminding them of the death of Christ on the cross (1 Cor. 11:26). The Lord's Table was the altar around which they worshiped, the antitype for which the ancient altar of burnt offerings had been the type. As the altar of burnt offerings pointed forward to the death of Christ on the cross, so the Lord's Supper points back to the same great event. It was here around this altar that they remembered their Lord's death and made their vows anew.

4. It was *devotional*. They sang together the ''psalms and hymns and spiritual songs'' of Zion and lifted their hearts to the Lord in thanksgiving and praise.

5. Here is a fourfold program divinely given, and we neglect it to our own hurt. Can any one hope to live a successful Christian life who continually cuts himself off from all these provisions for his spiritual life and growth?

C. *There is grave danger in neglecting to thus assemble ourselves together.*

We are exhorted in Heb. 10:22-25 to draw near to the Lord with true hearts, and not to forsake our own assembling together. In verses 26-31 the author points out the danger we are in if we fail to live the life we have begun, and there is a very close connection between *neglecting to assemble ourselves* and finally incurring the wrath of God. Those who willfully turn their backs upon the teaching of the Word, the fellowship of the church, the Lord's Supper and the prayers of Christians assembled together have in reality ''trodden underfoot the Son of God, and hath counted the blood of the covenant wherewith they were sanctified an unholy thing, and hath done despite unto the Spirit of grace.''

Lesson V

THE LORD'S SUPPER

I. The Atonement Is the Central Fact of History and Has a Prominent Place in the Teachings of Both the Old and New Testaments.

A. *The ordinances of the Old Testament are typical of great truths in the New.*

1. The Jewish tabernacle was "a figure [type] for the time present" (Heb. 9:1-9). The tabernacle with its furnishings was never meant to be a permanent institution, but was an institution of "carnal ordinances, imposed until a time of reformation" (Heb. 9:10).

2. In Heb. 9:23 the tabernacle and its furnishings are called "copies of things in the heavens." They were meant to picture to man what God had in mind concerning the coming kingdom.

3. Again the author of the Hebrew letter tells us that the law had "a shadow of good things to come," and he insists that since the law has only the shadow, "and not the very image of those things," it can not make perfect those that draw near by it (Heb. 10:1).

4. A careful study of the entire ninth chapter of the Hebrew letter, with especial attention given to 9:9, 10, 23 and 10:1, will reveal the fact that the ordinances of the Old Testament, including the ritual and the law of Moses, were typical of great truths in the New Testament.

B. *Many of the ordinances of the Old Testament pointed unmistakably to the shedding of the atoning blood of Christ upon the cross.*

1. The altar of burnt offerings (Ex. 27:1-8; Numbers 28) pointed directly to the sacrificial death of Christ. It is plain from Heb. 9:11-28 that the blood of the animal sacrifices was typical of the blood of Christ, and that the many animals slain in their feasts and regular worship were so many pictures of the coming crucifixion of Christ.

2. The Passover, the greatest of all Jewish feasts, pointed once each year to the sacrificial death of Christ, the Lamb of God slain from the foundation of the world (Ex. 12:1-28; 1 Cor. 5:7b).

3. The two goats of Lev. 16:5, 20-22 direct our attention to the twofold work of redemption wrought in the death of Christ. (a) On the one hand, Christ meets the requirements of a righteous and just God. Blood represents life, and for some reason unknown to us the justice of God demanded life as a ransom, and so only in the shedding of blood could there be remission of sins (Lev. 17:11; Heb. 9:22; Rom. 3:21-26). (b) On the other hand, Christ becomes the scapegoat that bears away the sins of the world (Isa. 53:6, 12; John 1:29). Thus Christ, in His death, satisfied both the justice and the mercy of God. He, the perfect man, became the perfect sacrifice satisfying the justice of God, and at the same time bore away the sins of the people, making possible their forgiveness. And so in the ordinance of the two goats we see the figure or type of Christ in the atonement.

C. *The table of showbread of the Old Testament quite clearly typified the table of the Lord in the New Testament.*

1. It had bread upon it (Lev. 24:5-8), and bread represents Christ's body in the Lord's Supper.

2. It had bowls, or flagons, which doubtless contained wine (Ex. 25:29, 30), and the fruit of the vine represents Christ's blood in the Lord's Supper.

3. The meaning of "showbread" is "bread of the face" or "bread of the presence," and Christ is always present in any proper observance of the Lord's Supper. He has promised to be with even two or three who meet in His name (Matt. 18:20), and He has indicated that He would eat with His disciples in His coming kingdom (Matt. 26:29), and we are inclined to believe He had reference to the church. Thus the table of showbread of the Old Testament prefigures or pictures the Lord's Supper in the New Testament.

II. The Lord's Supper of the New Testament Memorializes the Atonement.

A. *The great, outstanding event towards which the verbal prophecies and ordinances of the Old Testament pointed is not left without its witness in the New Testament,* but memorialized in a divinely given institution known today as the Lord's Supper.

1. Jesus, the divine Son of God, personally instituted it before His crucifixion (Matt. 26:26-29; Mark 14:22-25; Luke 22:19, 20).

2. It is to be observed in memory of a divine person, Jesus, the Christ of God (Luke 22:19; 1 Cor. 11:23-25).

B. *The Lord's Supper is essentially a New Testament institution.*

1. When Jesus instituted the Lord's Supper He declared He would not eat it again until He ate it anew with them in His Father's kingdom (Matt. 26:29). While He may have referred to the time when they would all partake of it in heaven, it is also conceivable that He had reference to the church and His own personal spiritual presence in the communion service in the church.

2. Of one thing we are sure, and that is that the Lord's Supper did become a definite ordinance of the church after the day of Pentecost (Acts 2:42; 20:7).

Page 34

C. *These ordinances of the Old Testament, which were types of the atonement and the Lord's Supper in the New Testament, were observed regularly.*

1. In the types of the atonement and of the Lord's Supper in the Old Testament the teaching of constancy may be seen: (a) The fire on the altar of burnt offerings, which was typical of the sacrifice of Christ, was to be kept burning day and night continually (Lev. 6:12, 13). (b) The Passover, which pointed to the work of deliverance through Christ, was to be observed each year throughout the history of Israel (Ex. 12: 37-42). (c) The table of showbread, which was typical of the Lord's Supper, was to be replenished every week (Lev. 24:8). If these types mean anything at all, they teach without doubt that the Lord's Supper should be observed regularly, and, to correspond with its exact type, the table of showbread, it must be observed every week.

D. *The New Testament is not less specific and plain in its teaching of constancy and regularity.*

1. That the early church practiced meeting regularly upon the first day of the week there can be no doubt. (a) Paul, in his first letter to the Corinthians, instructed them to lay by them in store upon the first day of the week for the Lord's work (1 Cor. 16:2). His reason for specifying *the first day of the week* was doubtless because they were in the habit of meeting on that day, and the place for storing the Lord's money would be available then. (b) But this was not only true of the church at Corinth, for he had given the same instructions to the churches of Galatia (1 Cor. 16:1). Paul had organized a number of churches in the province of Galatia, and it would seem that they also were meeting regularly upon the first day of the week.

2. Not only is it true that they came together regularly on the first day of the week, but it is also evident that they observed the Lord's Supper when they came together. (a) On one of his great evangelistic tours Paul met with a group of

the disciples at Troas for the specific purpose of partaking of the Lord's Supper. On his way to Jerusalem he had himself tarried in Macedonia, with Luke as his companion, while a number of his followers had gone on to Troas. After Paul joined them, although he was anxious to get to Jerusalem before the day of Pentecost (Acts 20: 13-16), he tarried in Troas seven days (Acts 20: 6), doubtless for the purpose of observing the Lord's Supper. (b) When they met on the first day of the week the record plainly tells us that it was for the purpose of breaking bread, or partaking of the Lord's Supper (Acts 20: 7). (c) Paul accuses the Corinthian church of coming together for the wrong purpose in that they have not come together to eat the Lord's Supper (1 Cor. 11: 20). We may conclude from this that the purpose for which they should have come together was to eat the Lord's Supper.

3. Since they were in the habit of coming together every first day of the week (1 Cor. 16: 1, 2), and since the purpose of this coming together was to break bread (Acts 20: 1-7; 1 Cor. 11: 20), we may safely conclude that they observed the Lord's Supper every Lord's Day: (a) Acts 2: 42 strengthens this teaching. In this passage we have a complete program of worship—"apostles' teaching . . . fellowship in the Lord's work . . . the breaking of bread and the prayers"—all of which indicates that it was a Lord's Day service, and in this worship service they did not neglect the Lord's Supper. (b) The teaching of Heb. 10: 19-31 has a greater depth of meaning when we consider that in assembling themselves together they would also partake of the Lord's Supper.

III. The Lord's Supper Should Be Worthily Observed.

A. *The Lord's Supper is not a so-called "love feast," with feet washing a necessary part of it.*

1. Feet washing and the institution of the Lord's Supper did not occur at the same time as is practiced by those who

Page 36

wash feet today. Jesus washed His disciples' feet *before* the Passover (John 13:1-17), while the Lord's Supper was instituted at the close of the Passover supper (Luke 22:1-23).

2. Divine ordinances are always closely related to the most essential facts of the plan of salvation: (a) Immersion commemorates the burial and resurrection of Jesus, the death of the old man of sin in us, and the resurrection of the new man to walk in newness of life (Rom. 6:1-4). (b) The Lord's Supper memorializes the death of Christ on the cross (1 Cor. 11:26), the central fact of the gospel. (c) Feet washing is in no way vitally connected with the plan of salvation and could not possibly take the status of an ordinance.

3. That feet washing is not an ordinance of the church is evident from the fact that it was never practiced by the church of the apostles. The apostolic church was directed by apostles, who were themselves inspired and guided by the Holy Spirit (Acts 1:6-8), and if feet washing had been divinely authorized as a practice of the future church, it would have been observed by that church.

4. The Lord's Supper is not to be observed as a physical feast. The trouble with the Corinthian church was that they had converted a memorial ordinance into a feast of revelry (1 Cor. 11:17-22). It can be a feast only insofar as it feeds the soul.

B. *Only Christians have a right to this memorial table.*

1. The Jew, as such, has no right to this table (Heb. 13:10).

2. The one who has never accepted Christ as his Lord and Saviour has no right to this ordinance. He belongs to the world and serves the wrong master. This is the Lord's Table and only the Lord's people have a right to it (1 Cor. 10:21).

3. And yet we, as Christians, can not exclude any who come. It is not our table, but the Lord's. He invites and rejects whom He will, and we have nothing to do with the matter.

C. *In partaking of the Lord's Supper each one must "prove," "judge" or "examine" himself.*

1. We have no right to judge our fellow men (Matt. 7:1). The neighbor who sits by your side in the communion service may be living in sin, but you are not communing with him; you are communing with the Lord; moreover, we can not be sure that our judgment is correct in any given case, for we are human and make many mistakes. Only the Lord is capable of judging who is and who is not fit to partake of the Lord's Supper.

2. Each one, however, should carefully examine himself: (a) He should not come with hatred in his heart for any one (1 John 2:9). (b) He should not come with enmity which he can prevent between him and his brother, or with any unforgiven sin against his brother upon his soul (Matt. 5: 23, 24). (c) He should come, not in a spirit of self-righteousness such as the Pharisee had in the story of the Pharisee and the publican (Luke 18:9-14), but he should come in an humble spirit confessing his sins (1 John 1:8, 9).

D. *This memorial should be observed reverently.*

1. It is the communion of the body and blood of the Lord (1 Cor. 10:16). Not that the bread and the fruit of the vine is the *actual* body and blood of the Lord, as the Roman Catholics teach (all the senses—and, we may add, all the sense of man—teaches to the contrary), but here is that which forcibly reminds us of His death and our own participation in the benefits of that death. Thus only can we eat His flesh and drink His blood. How grateful we should be for His sacrifice, and how sacred should be these moments when we are privileged to commemorate this great event!

2. It is a time of great solemnity. This memorial was instituted in the very shadow of the cross. The very night of His betrayal, the night in which He agonized in Gethsemane, and the night before His body was nailed to the cross, "Jesus took bread, and blessed, and brake it; and he gave it to his

disciples, and said, Take, eat; this is my body. And he took the cup, and gave thanks, and gave to them, saying, Drink ye all of it; for this is my blood of the covenant, which is poured out for many unto remission of sins'' (Matt. 26:26-28).

3. It is a funeral occasion. It is observed in memory of His death (1 Cor. 11:26). We would not think of dishonoring the most unworthy of our friends and neighbors by light jesting or any kind of unbecoming conduct at his funeral, but many times we dishonor the Lord by our thoughtlessness at the time that His death is being commemorated.

IV. Conclusions.

A. *There are a few definite conclusions to which we have come in our study of this subject which we summarize in this last paragraph.*

1. That the Lord's Supper has to do with the most important and vital fact of the Christian religion and of human history, and is closely related to all the prophecies concerning the atonement for man's sins in the death of Christ upon the cross.

2. That it should be observed every first day of the week, and that to fail to observe is to incur grave danger to our souls.

3. That each one should carefully examine his own heart in partaking of it.

4. That it should be observed earnestly, solemnly and reverently.

THE INDWELLING SPIRIT

Introductory Remarks: In this lesson we shall not enter the realm of disputed questions among us on the subject of the Holy Spirit, but confine ourselves to that phase of the subject upon which we are generally agreed; namely, the indwelling presence of the Holy Spirit. It shall'be the purpose of this lesson to help us to realize that we may, and should, have this Spirit as our helper in an increasing measure as we grow in the Christian life.

I. The Christian Dispensation Is the Dispensation of the Holy Spirit.

A. *The old or Jewish covenant was a covenant of law.*

1. God's people were kept in ward under the law until Christ should come (Gal. 3:23). They were in bondage to the law through fear of death (Heb. 2:15), and were governed by this spirit of fear rather than the spirit of Christ residing within. The highest type of manhood could not be achieved until man was freed from this bondage, controlled by an earnest desire from within, rather than an exacting law without.

2. The time came when men worshiped God in spirit and in truth (John 4:19-24), and the old shackles of fear fell away. Ours is now to be a spiritual worship rather than a formal submission to law.

3. The new covenant which you and I have entered into with the Lord is not the following of a rigid law to the letter as did the Jews, but a covenant wherein we surrender to the gentle wooing of the Holy Spirit and render warm-hearted and willing service to our King. Worship, service or life that is produced by formal compliance with the law only, even though it measures up to the very letter of the law, brings only a dead state, but the free expression of the indwelling Spirit shining through our lives brings us into the "more abundant life."

B. *Jesus promised the coming of the Holy Spirit in a manner that was different from that of any former dispensation.*

1. This Spirit had been present on various occasions in the patriarchal and Jewish dispensations, but His stay had apparently lasted only until His mission was accomplished. He was present in the creation of the world (Gen. 1:2). He was present in the performance of many miracles in those ages, and certain individuals were said to be filled with the Spirit, such as Joseph (Gen. 41:38), Joshua (Num. 27:18), David (Ps. 51:11), and many others, but yet in the days of Christ's earthly ministry there was a sense in which the Holy Spirit had not come.

2. His coming in this different way was of such value and importance that Jesus said that it was expedient, or best, for His disciples that He go away, for if He did not go away, the Spirit would not come (John 16:7).

3. Earlier in Christ's ministry John had said that the Holy Spirit was not yet given, and indicated that He would not be given until Jesus was glorified (John 7:38, 39). Thus we may see that, while He had been active in the affairs of the world before, there was a different sense in which He was yet to come.

C. *Certain distinct characteristics of His coming in the Christian dispensation are plainly taught in the Scriptures.*

1. He was coming to guide. The apostles would especially need this guidance as they, for the first time, told men what to do to be saved, and laid the foundation for the future church. The writers of the gospel records would need this guidance as they produced the books of the New Testament. The early Christians would need it as they met the opposition of the foes of the gospel and endured the fiery trials through which they were to pass. Nor should we make the mistake of assuming that the Spirit no longer guides men, since the days of miracles are past. On the contrary, there is a sense in which the Spirit still guides men, as will be shown briefly a little later.

2. He was coming to testify of Christ (John 15:26; 16:13, 14). This work was accomplished at first through inspired men (Acts 1:8), the Holy Spirit bearing witness to the truth of their words by many signs and wonders (Mark 16:20; Acts 5:12; 1 Cor. 2:4, 5; Heb. 2:4). Other men, such as Philip and Stephen, although not inspired in the same sense as the apostles, were doubtless assisted by the direct presence of the Spirit in bringing their messages and testimony for Christ. After the days of the apostles the Word, inspired by the Holy Spirit, was the source of testimony for Christ.

3. He was coming to convict the world of sin, righteousness and judgment (John 16:7, 8). The need of the world then was, and still is, conviction—conviction of its own sin, of the righteousness of Christ and of judgment. The work of the Holy Spirit was to appeal to the intellect, rather than the emotions; to convict, or convince, rather than to touch emotionally.

4. He was coming to abide forever (John 14:15-17). The person of the patriarchal dispensation was Abraham; the person of the Jewish dispensation was Moses; in the Christian dispensation the guiding and abiding person is the Holy Spirit; thus we may think of this dispensation as being distinctly the dispensation of the Spirit.

Page 42

II. This Indwelling Spirit May Be the Possession of Every True Christian (Rom. 8:9).

A. *Many passages of Scripture indicate that this is true.*

1. Both Paul and John declare He has given us the Spirit (1 John 3:24; 4:13; Rom. 5:5).

2. Paul also tells us that our bodies are temples of the Holy Spirit (1 Cor. 6:15-20).

B. *We receive this Holy Spirit through obedience and prayer.*

1. Peter promised it to those who would repent and be baptized (Acts 2:38). This promise was not limited to those whom he was then addressing, nor yet to the apostolic age, but was "for all them that are afar off, even as many as the Lord shall call unto him" (Acts 2:39).

2. Peter told the Jewish council that the Lord had given the Holy Spirit to "them that obey him" (Acts 5:32).

3. While we receive the Holy Spirit at the time of our new birth through obedience, we may have this Spirit in increasing measure through asking, or through prayer (Luke 11:13).

C. *This Spirit may also be banished from our lives.*

1. He may be grieved because of our failure to live a faithful and loyal Christian life (Eph. 4:30). The Spirit will not long abide in a life filled with sin.

2. He may also be insulted, or even blasphemed, because of our failure to follow the Lord (Matt. 12:31, 32; Heb. 10:19-29). When we have once known the power of the Spirit in our lives, and then turn away from Him, we insult Him. Can we expect Him to abide with us under such treatment?

3. We also have the power to "quench" this Spirit (1 Thess. 5:19). We can quench Him by filling our lives with sin and worldliness. We can stifle every holy emotion and impulse, and willfully live a life of selfishness and sin; and, if we do this, He will surely depart from us.

D. *If allowed to remain in our hearts, this Spirit will work great blessings in our lives.*

He will bear rich fruit in our lives. If He is allowed to abide within us, we will produce such fruit as love, joy, peace, longsuffering, kindness, goodness, faithfulness, meekness and self-control. One who has this indwelling Spirit is not under the law, because there is no law, either human or divine, against such fruits as these.

B. *This indwelling Spirit will guide us in life.* James reminds us that we do not have complete control of our lives, but that we must take the Lord into consideration in making plans for the future (Jas. 4:13-15). Paul exhorts us to "walk by the Spirit" (Gal. 5:16) and be transformed by the Spirit (2 Cor. 3:17, 18). This Spirit led men in the days of the apostles (Acts 8:26-31; 9:10-16; 10:9-20, 30-33; 16: 6-9). Is there any good reason to believe that He will not continue to lead men today? It is true that He does not lead us in any miraculous way, but we can safely commit our way unto Him. He will not deprive us of our own responsibility and self-determination, but many times our plans may be overruled for our good and the Lord's own good purposes.

III. As Christians, We Should Seek to Live by the Spirit.

The eighth chapter of the Roman letter gives us some splendid teaching upon this subject that should not be overlooked.

A. *Only those who walk by the Spirit fulfill the requirements of righteousness* (vs. 1-4).

1. These fulfill the righteousness for which the law of Moses stood, and then go far beyond that which the law required. Spirit-filled men go the second mile. They do all that the law ever required, and go beyond that law, bringing forth the rich fruit of the Spirit.

2. The mind of the flesh can not fulfill this purpose because it is unwilling to submit, or "is not subject to the

Page 44

law of God.'' There is a constant war going on between the flesh and the Spirit, and these two can not be in agreement (vs. 5-8).

B. *If we are truly Christians, we sustain very close relationship to this indwelling Spirit.*

1. We are in Him and He is in us (v. 9). He is not just a temporary power that performs some particular work and then departs, but He is a close, intimate and abiding presence in our lives at all times as a Helper and Guide.

2. It is this indwelling Spirit that keeps us alive (vs. 13, 14). To live for the gratification of the flesh is to be ''carnally-minded,'' and ''to be carnally-minded is death'' (v. 6). The branch must remain in the vine to live, and we must remain in the Spirit or suffer spiritual death. By this indwelling Spirit we sustain vital contact with Him.

3. This indwelling Spirit is an evidence of our sonship (vs. 16, 17). His continued presence assures us that we belong to Christ, for only those who belong to Him can have this Holy Spirit. He was never promised to any one else.

4. This indwelling Spirit makes intercession for us (vs. 26, 27). We are not always capable of knowing how to pray, but the Spirit takes our faltering, stumbling words and translates them to the Father, adding what we have left out and taking away what should not be said.

5. This indwelling Spirit will be the power that will raise us from the dead (v. 11). When the seed is buried beneath the soil it is the germ of life that causes it to sprout and push through the crust above it. When Jesus was buried in Joseph's new tomb He came forth from the dead without any assistance from the outside. If you and I are raised from the dead in the final day, it will be because of the life that is within, and not because of any outside power compelling us or even assisting us.

May we pray earnestly that we may have this great and wonderful Holy Spirit in an increasing way in our hearts.

YOUR PRAYER LIFE

I. Every Christian Should Learn to Pray Well.

While one may assimilate some spiritual food from contact with spiritual life, in the services of the church, from the reading of the Bible and from association with spiritually minded Christians, yet the greatest source of spiritual food remains unused unless we learn to pray.

A. *Perfect though He was, Jesus felt the need of constant prayer* and communion with His Father, and every important event and decision of His life was safeguarded and sanctified in prayer.

1. At the very beginning of His public ministry, as He dedicated Himself to God in baptism, He prayed (Luke 3: 21). What a splendid example for all those who are baptized today!

2. When He would choose twelve men who were to be His apostles and finally the instruments by which He would establish His kingdom, He spent an entire night in prayer (Luke 6: 12, 13).

3. After the feeding of the five thousand and before rescuing His disciples at sea, He went into the mountain to pray alone (Matt. 14: 13-33).

4. At the conclusion of His parting message to His apostles just before His crucifixion He "lifted up his eyes to heaven" and prayed earnestly on behalf of all His followers (John 17).

Page 46

5. At the institution of the Lord's Supper, which should memorialize His death and remind succeeding generations of the precious gift of His atoning blood, He did not forget to pray (Mark 14: 22, 23).

6. Just before the final ordeal of His arrest and crucifixion He took three of His disciples and went into the Garden of Gethsemane to agonize in prayer (Matt. 26: 36-44).

7. And as He hung suspended upon the cross His dying lips were eloquent in prayer (Matt. 27: 46, 50; Luke 23: 34, 46; John 19: 30). If the Son of God, sinless and perfect, needed· to pray, how much more we need to do so!

B. *The apostolic church was a praying church.*

1. The church had its beginning in the midst of a protracted prayer meeting. After the ascension of our Lord, the apostles, together with many other disciples of Jesus, met daily in an upper room in Jerusalem, where they continued stedfastly in prayer. When the day of Pentecost came "they were all together in one place," doubtless for the purpose of prayer (Acts 1: 12—2: 1).

2. The church did not cease to pray after that wonderful day of Pentecost, but "they continued stedfastly in . . . the prayers" (Acts 2: 42).

3. When Peter was cast into prison by Herod the church was gathered together praying for his release (Acts 12: 1-13).

4. In taking leave of the elders at Ephesus, and likewise at Tyre, Paul kneeled down and prayed with them (Acts 20: 36; 21: 3-5).

If the church of today is to follow the pattern of the church in the New Testament, we will have to restore prayer to its proper place in the life of the church and in the lives of its members.

C. *The Christian needs prayer in the battle of life.*

1. He needs to pray to overcome the temptations of life. No man is sufficiently strong within himself to resist life's temptations. He must somehow be able to reach up and take

hold of a Power greater than his own. Prayer affords him the means by which he may take hold of God, who is abundantly able to help him fight his battles. After the bitter agony in Gethsemane Jesus returned, and for the third time found His disciples asleep. Seeing them thus, He warned them against temptations, saying, "Watch and pray, that ye enter not into temptation" (Matt. 26:41) We today need indeed to watch, but we need also to pray, lest we enter into temptations.

2. We need also to confess our faults in prayer. James recommends that we confess our "sins one to another and pray for one another, that ye may be healed" (Jas. 5:16), and John indicates that we need to make a confession of our sins to God in prayer (1 John 1:9).

3. We need also to pray for courage to go on in the battle of life. It is so easy for us to lose heart in the task and give up. One of the Master's greatest parables taught the lesson of perseverance in prayer (Luke 18:1-8).

4. There are many other passages of Scripture that emphasize the importance of prayer in our daily lives, such as 1 Thess. 5:17; 1 Tim. 2:8; Col. 4:2; Phil. 4:6; Eph. 6:18.

II. The Christian Has a Unique Privilege in Prayer.

A. *The Christian comes to God in prayer with the assurance that God will hear him.*

1. God has nowhere promised to hear the prayers of unrepentant sinners (1 Pet. 3:12) Whether or not God will make some exceptions to this general principle is not for us to say, or perhaps theorize upon, but we can be assured that if we are His we have an open door of access to Him in prayer.

2. The Lord has always heard, and will continue to hear, the prayers of those who belong to Him (Jas. 5:13-18; Matt. 21:22).

Page 48

B. *The way into the Holy of Holies has been "made manifest" (opened) by the death of Christ.*

1. When Jesus expired on the cross, the veil of the temple was rent in two from top to bottom (Matt. 27:51). The author of the Hebrew letter makes it plain that the veil of the temple, while yet not rent in two, indicated that the way into the Holy of Holies was not yet "made manifest," or opened, and that before Christ died only an imperfect high priest could enter into that sacred place, and at that only once a year, to make atonement for his own sins and the sins of the people, but that now, since Christ died, He has Himself, the perfect One, "entered in once for all, having obtained eternal redemption" (Heb. 9:6-12).

2. Paul is in perfect accord with this statement when he says that Jesus is now at the right hand of God, making intercession for us (Rom. 8:34).

3. Because we have sinned we are unworthy to stand in the presence of God, but Jesus, our great High Priest, "now appears before the face of God for us" (Heb. 7:24-28; 9: 24-26).

C. *The Christian may come boldly to the throne of grace.*

1. Jesus, our High Priest, can be touched by our weaknesses and sympathize with us when we are tempted, for "he was tempted in all points like as we are, yet without sin." It is through His intercession that I may come boldly (without fear) to the throne to receive mercy and pardon when I sin (Heb. 4:14-16).

2. Entrance into this holy place (of prayer) is made only through the blood of Jesus, and we are able to claim the benefits of His atoning blood only when our hearts have been sprinkled from an evil conscience and our bodies have been washed in pure water (Heb. 10:19-22). In other words, only those who have complied with the conditions of salvation can be assured that their prayers will be heard and that Jesus will intercede in their behalf.

III. There Are Certain Conditions of Heart that Are Essential to Effective Prayer.

A. *Humbleness is essential in prayer.*

1. Jesus condemned the Pharisees because "they trusted in themselves and set all others at naught," and He set forth a parable in which He declared that the humble man, even though he was a sinner, "went down to his house .justified rather than the other," who trusted in himself (Luke 18: 9-14). We need a sense of our own sin and unworthiness as we approach the throne of grace. Jesus taught His disciples to pray, "Forgive us our sins" (Matt. 6: 12).

2. Prayer should never become merely a parading before the public of our own goodness. Jesus declared that they who make a vain show of prayer "have received their reward" (Matt. 6: 5-8). They have received something of approval and commendation from men for their seeming piety, but that is the full extent of their benefit and reward. It is not wrong to pray in public, but effectual public prayer is learned on the knees in the "inner closets" of our lives, where we seek a closer walk with our Lord.

B. *The spirit of forgiveness is essential in prayer.*

1. Jesus warns us that the heavenly Father will not forgive us unless we forgive those who have wronged us (Mark 11: 24, 25; Matt. 6: 14, 15). How dare we come before the throne of grace with bitterness, envy and hatred in our hearts?

2. In one of His great parables Jesus presents a certain servant who, even though his master had forgiven him a great debt, would not forgive his fellow servant a very small one, but cast him into prison (Matt. 18: 23-35). How much that servant resembles many of us today!

3. It is essential that we maintain the *spirit* of forgiveness at all times. Peter wanted a legal statute limiting forgiveness to a specified number of times, but Jesus indicated that for-

Page 50

giveness could not be limited (Matt. 18:21, 22). We must strive to maintain the spirit of forgiveness at all times.

C. *Faith is essential to effective prayer.*

1. Because of their lack of faith the apostles were unable to cast out the demon (Matt. 17:20, 21).

2. Jesus said, "All things whatsoever ye pray and ask for, believe that ye receive them, and ye shall have them" (Mark 11:24).

3. James said, "The prayer of faith shall save the sick" (Jas. 5:15).

D. *The Holy Spirit must be present in our lives if our prayers are to be effective.*

1. "The Spirit maketh intercession for us," says Paul (Rom. 8:26). Our finest prayers would be wholly unfit to come before the throne of grace, but the Spirit takes our poor prayers and so presents them to the Father that they are acceptable unto Him. The prayer that does not have the stamp and approval of the Spirit will have a poor chance of being heard by the Almighty.

2. How can the Holy Spirit help us in prayer if we are not walking daily in the Spirit? We need Him in our hearts and lives daily, but we can only have Him there as we eliminate sins from our lives. Perhaps this is why James says that "the effectual, fervent prayer of a righteous man availeth much" (Jas. 5:16, K. J.).

3. With Jesus to intercede for us at the right hand of God, and with the Holy Spirit to intercede for us here, our poor prayers may come before the great throne of God, there to be accepted and answered according to His divine wisdom and mercy.

How gracious the privilege of prayer and how earnestly we ought to cultivate it!

YOUR PLACE IN THE CHURCH

Introduction: There is a place for every one who wishes to work in the New Testament plan of the church, and there is no need that we find ourselves idle if we follow that plan. We have, however, made two serious mistakes in the past.

A. *We have not properly evaluated and recognized our stewardship of talents.*

1. We all possess some talents. Jesus, in a somewhat general classification, indicates in His parable of the talents that one may have five, two or one talents, and that these talents are to be used for the Lord (Matt. 25 : 14-30). Too often we do not recognize God's ownership and our own stewardship in the matter of talents.

2. The members of the first church at Jerusalem recognized their stewardship, at least in material things, for "not one of them said that aught of the things that he possessed was his own" (Acts 4 : 32). When we have come to recognize all our possessions as things which have been entrusted to us for the Master's use, we will have attained a proper estimate of our stewardship.

3. In the final analysis we do not own ourselves, because we have been purchased by the blood of Jesus (1 Cor. 6 : 20). All that we have, whether of money or ability, belongs to the Lord. The Lord does not want us to turn it back to Him, as did the man with the one talent, but to use it for His glory in His service.

B. *Our second great mistake lies in the fact that we have not always been content to follow the plan of the New Testament.* While the New Testament should not be thought of as a set of rigid rules in this matter, it does furnish us with a program of church work that will employ every worker, and it is doubtful if we have been wise in so frequently going beyond, and so far beyond in some cases, the simple procedure of the church of the New Testament.

1. In some instances we have "gone to seed" on organization. Separate organizations are formed for every little task in the church. In many churches we have multiplied organizations until it is very difficult to see the church around which they are organized. It is true that we need organization for effective work in any field, but in the field of religion the New Testament furnishes a plan of organization which, while quite simple, will be sufficient for most, if not all, our needs.

2. We fall short of the purpose and spirit of the New Testament when we substitute church suppers, ice-cream socials and other commercial projects for the Scriptural method of finance. Every man, woman and child in the church can be employed in the more vital work and life of the church, and the services of the church will be enriched, the attendance will increase, the needy will be helped and souls will be won to Christ if only we could engage the whole church more directly in the main task. In the outline which follows it will be discovered that there is ample opportunity for all who wish to serve in the New Testament plan.

I. There Is a Place for Many to Work in the Evangelistic Program of the Church.

So long as there is a single soul unsaved the supreme task of the church will be evangelism.

A. *There is then a place in the New Testament plan for evangelists.*

1. The Great Commission, although originally given to the apostles, was not confined to them, but was recognized as the task of the whole church. Thus not only the apostles, but Philip, Stephen, Barnabas, Apollos, Timothy and others were soon employed in that important phase of church work.

2. If the church of today is to continue to carry out this commission, there must be those who will "do the work of an evangelist" (2 Tim. 4:5). In every church there are young men and young women who should be planning to give themselves in full-time Christian service in the field of evangelism.

B. *There is also a place for personal evangelists in the New Testament plan.*

1. The members of the church at Jerusalem, not the apostles and evangelists alone, when the churches were scattered by persecution, "went everywhere preaching the word" (Acts 8:4). And those who thus went out under bitter persecution preaching the Word, must have been earnest proclaimers of that Word in the home church at Jerusalem, or they would not have continued to preach it under such circumstances.

2. There has always been a scarcity of laborers in the harvest field of the Lord (Luke 10:2). We will never have too many preachers while there are lands that have never heard the gospel and vast areas practically untouched. And we will never have too many personal evangelists in any local church so long as there are unsaved souls in that community.

3. If you want to shine, not as some bright light here, but as an unobtrusive star in God's eternal firmament, begin now to turn men to righteousness (Dan. 12:3).

II. There Is a Place for Church Officers in the New Testament Plan.

A. *The New Testament recognized the office of the eldership.*

1. There were elders in the church at Jerusalem to whom Paul and Barnabas brought the question of controversy in the church at Antioch (Acts 15:1-31).

2. Paul and Barnabas appointed elders in the churches they had organized (Acts 14:23).

3. Paul called for the elders of the church at Ephesus on his way to Jerusalem (Acts 20:28-30).

4. Paul gives the qualifications of an elder in his letters to Timothy and Titus (1 Tim. 3:1-7; Tit. 1:5-9).

B. *To be an ideal elder one must have many qualifications.*

Since it is not the purpose of this lesson to treat extensively the question of the eldership, we will have to confine ourselves here to merely listing those qualifications.

1. From Paul's letter to Timothy we have the following: Without reproach, the husband of one wife, sober-minded, orderly, temperate, given to hospitality, apt to teach, no brawler, no striker, gentle, not contentious, no lover of money, one that ruleth well his own house, having his children in subjection with all gravity, not a novice and having a good testimony from them that are without (1 Tim. 3:1-7).

2. From Paul's letter to Titus we have the following additional requirements: Just, holy, a lover of good and holding to the faithful word.

3. While no one will perhaps measure up to all the qualifications, yet we must use this standard as our measuring rod in the selection of elders, and, if one aspires to become an elder, let him measure himself by this standard, and seek to reach its requirements.

C. *The functions of the elders are the general care of the local congregations, especially in spiritual matters.*

1. They are to teach the congregation (1 Tim. 4:11).

2. They are the *overseers* of the church. The word *bishop,* as used in 1 Tim. 3:1 and elsewhere, is from the Greek word *episcopas,* which means "overseer."

3. In a limited sense they are the rulers of the church (Heb. 13:17). They were not to "lord it over" the church, but were to "tend the flock" and "have the oversight of it" (1 Pet. 5:1-3).

D. *The office of elder was one to be desired* (1 Tim. 3:1).

1. The qualifications for an elder, according to the New Testament, constitute a goal worth striving for. When one is able to measure up to any great portion of those qualifications he may think of himself in complimentary terms. To desire then to be an elder according to the New Testament requirements is indeed to "desire a good thing."

2. We need more young men today who will learn to dream of the day when they will qualify as elders in the church of Christ.

E. *The New Testament also recognizes the office of deacons.*

1. Paul gives us the qualifications for deacons in 1 Tim. 3:8-13, which constitutes a New Testament recognition of the office.

2. The church at Jerusalem had its deacons in the seven men who were selected to have charge of the daily distributions from the common fund of the disciples there (Acts 6:1-6).

3. While the office of deacon may be filled by men with fewer talents than that of the eldership, it is by no means an unimportant office. The qualifications are almost as exacting, and their work is very similar to that of the elders. The men who were selected as deacons by the church at Jerusalem were men who were "filled with the spirit," and at least two of them, Philip and Stephen, were great leaders in the work of the early church. Paul gives the following qualifications for deacons: "grave, not double-tongued, not given to much wine, not greedy of filthy lucre; holding the mystery of the faith in a pure conscience. . . . husbands of one wife, and ruling well their own houses" (1 Tim. 3:8-13).

III. There Is a Place in the Worship Services of the Church of the New Testament for Many to Help.

A. *The New Testament recognizes the place and need of singing as a part of the worship,* and there are many who can sing. Let not your talent for singing be despised in your own

Page 56

eyes, for it can be used to bless others and to bring you great joy in the service you can render.

1. Singing may be a means of teaching. Paul recommends that we admonish and teach one another in songs (Col. 3 : 16). The gospel may be sung much more effectively sometimes than it is preached or taught in a Bible-school class. There is need today for those who will exercise care and discrimination in the selection of songs for congregational or other singing, for there is much of teaching value as well as something of false teaching in our songbooks.

2. Singing may also be a means of spiritual communication one with another, for we may "speak to one another in" songs (Eph. 5 : 19).

3. Singing may be a means of imparting cheer to ourselves and others. Paul and Silas sang songs with their feet in the stocks, and James admonishes us to sing when we are cheerful (Jas. 5 : 13). There are few things more cheering than to hear some happy soul singing with freedom and abandon the great songs of Zion.

B. *The New Testament plan of church worship provides a place for those to serve who can pray,* even though they may not have talents for any other service. And prayer is one of the very greatest services that can be rendered in the church. That church is indeed fortunate that can number among its members those who can pray well.

1. "Prayer is the key that opens heaven's door." The prayer meeting and prayer service in the church are the means of linking the church with God. Without prayer the church will be powerless to serve in any great way.

2. Prayer is a means of edifying those who are present in the service. In the fourteenth chapter of 1 Corinthians Paul contends that if one should pray in an unknown tongue, those who could not understand the tongue would not be edified (1 Cor. 14 : 13-19). May we not, therefore, logically conclude that those who pray well in public will edify those present?

IV. Finally, There Is a Place in the New Testament Plan of the Church for Loving Ministrations.

A. *The church should become more of a ministering, and less of a begging, institution.* The church of today needs to take the position of a giver rather than a receiver of good things.

1. "Pure religion and undefiled before God" will include ministering to the needy (Jas. 1:27). We must learn the joy that comes from loving service in the name of Christ.

2. The officers of the church do not hold positions of ruiership, but rather of loving ministration.

3. When James writes about "faith without works" being dead (Jas. 2:14-17), he is writing about faith that ministers to the needy.

4. Ministering to the needs of others is ministering to Christ (Matt. 25:31-46). We can not serve Christ with our means. He has no need for our money or gifts, for all things are His, but when we minister to others who are in need we are serving Him.

5. Love is the greatest of all talents. Not gifts of eloquent speech, not great knowledge, not an understanding of the future, not even great faith, but great love is the greatest of all talents (1 Corinthians 13). When all other talents have failed, love will many times succeed. Somehow a wise and merciful heavenly Father has so arranged matters that the greatest of all gifts or talents is easily within the reach of the humblest of His disciples, for there is no one so poor that he can not love his fellow men.

IV. Conclusion.

Let us not despair of a place of real service in the church, for there are many important tasks which we can do; but let us be willing to say, as did Paul, "Lord, what wilt thou have me to do?"

YOU AND YOUR MONEY

I. The Law of Christian Giving Is a Fundamental Necessity as Well as a Divine Requirement.

As a matter of fact, any divine law is a law because it is a fundamental necessity, but we are discussing here the subject of Christian giving and shall confine ourselves to the law of giving.

A. *Giving is a necessity to the one who gives.*

If your life is to be a selfish one, if you are always getting and never giving, you can have little of blessing from the Lord.

1. It is by giving that we receive. "Give and it shall be given unto you," said Jesus (Luke 6:38). When we have learned to open our hearts to the needs of others we will have fellowship with Jesus in a wonderful and blessed ministry, for His life was a life of giving. We may not be blessed materially by giving, but great spiritual blessings may be ours. It is a bit unworthy of us to think always of material blessings. It is not a very high motive to think, because we have given a dollar to some good cause, that somehow we are going to get a dollar and a half back. The Lord has promised to care for the needs of those who serve Him, but the greatest blessings in Christian giving are spiritual rather than material.

2. "They that sow sparingly shall reap also sparingly" (2 Cor. 9:6). There can never be any great richness of spiritual blessing in a life that is too careful of its own interests. Even in material things one may be too close-fisted to make any money, and this is true to an even greater extent in the spiritual realm. Read Prov. 11:24, 25.

B. *Giving is also a necessity to the one who receives.*

1. There are in our land, and in many other lands, great numbers of people who for some cause are in need. This has always been and always will be true. Jesus spoke no idle word when He said, "The poor you have always with you" (Matt. 26:11). Distributing to the necessity of the poor is a positive, divine command (Rom. 12:13), and it will not excuse us to say that they are unworthy or unappreciative. As a rule people are appreciative of assistance rendered. They may not always express their appreciation, and there may be some exceptions to the general rule, but the rule holds nevertheless.

2. Christian giving is a necessity to the maintenance of the church. The church is dependent upon the proclaiming of the gospel for its very existence. It not only exists *to* preach the gospel, but it also exists *by* preaching the gospel. The church that ceases to preach the gospel has ceased to fulfill its mission, and will in most cases die, and it ought to die. The Lord's plan, although to men it may seem foolish, is to save men by the preaching of the gospel (1 Cor. 1:21). If then the church is to save men by the preaching of the gospel, men must be sent out by the church to preach, for "How shall they preach, except they be sent?" (Rom. 10:14, 15); and the church that sends them out is surely responsible for their maintenance. In Paul's estimation, the one who preaches the gospel has a right to live of the gospel (1 Cor. 9:7-14), which means that the church is under obligation to support its ministry in material necessities, while its ministry labors for it in spiritual things.

Page 60

II. The Tithe Should Be Taken as the Minimum, But Not the Maximum, of Christian Giving.

A. *The Scriptures do not require us to give everything we have to the church.*

1. Jesus promised something of earthly as well as eternal reward (Mark 10:29, 30), and Paul declares that "godliness is profitable . . . for the life that now is," as well as "that which is to come" (1 Tim. 4:8).

2. It is a positive sin to neglect one's own family (1 Tim. 5:8). The Lord has never required anything unreasonable of man, and He certainly does not require us to give to the extent of impoverishing our own loved ones. If, however, we give in the Lord's way, and He has a way, He will see to it that we lack nothing we need in this life.

B. *The Scriptures recommend proportionate giving,* or giving based upon what we receive.

1. Jesus taught that a part of our possessions belongs to God, just as a part belongs to Cæsar or to the government (Matt. 22:21). We recognize the right of the government to levy taxes because it protects and benefits us. Is it not true that the Lord protects and provides for us much more? And if so, is it not right that He should expect a part of our income?

2. Our giving to the Lord should be systematic. Too often our giving is haphazard and spasmodic. Paul recommended to the churches of Galatia and at Corinth an ideal plan of giving (1 Cor. 16:1, 2).

(a) According to this plan, giving should be regular, or at stated times—"upon the first day of the week." The New Testament plan for the church and for the individual Christian in the church encourages regular habits of worship and service, such as regular attendance and observance of the Lord's Supper, praying and reading the Bible. It is not less clear in the matter of regularity in our giving.

(b) According to this plan, giving should also be personal, or individualistic—"let every one of you." No one who has become a child of God has a right to try to shift the responsibility of giving to some one else. The greatest means of spiritual development and joy is denied the wife and children when the father mistakenly assumes all responsibility in the matter of giving.

(c) This plan is also based upon sound economic principles and encourages the habit of saving or "laying by him in store."

(d) This plan provides for proportionate giving—"as God hath prospered him."

C. *The tithe was the divinely ordained proportion under all former dispensations,* and as such commends itself to our serious consideration.

1. It was used as a standard of giving in the days of the patriarchs. Abraham paid the tithe to Melchizedek (Gen. 14: 17-20), and Jacob vowed to pay the tithe to the Lord (Gen. 28: 20-22).

2. The tithe became a part of the law given from Mt. Sinai (Lev. 27: 30), and was observed by the Hebrews throughout their history. It was still a part of their practices during the days of Christ (Matt. 23: 23).

D. *The Christian should not give less, but more, than did God's people in any former dispensation.*

1. He is living under a better covenant and enjoys better promises than they enjoyed (Heb. 8: 6; 11: 40).

2. Jesus raised rather than lowered the standards of life for the Christian (Matt. 5: 21, 22, 43, 44). If He raised the standard here, are we not safe in concluding that He raised it also in the matter of giving?

3: If the Jew should go beyond the tithe (Luke 11: 42), how can we as Christians, living under the new covenant with all its blessings, promises and privileges, excuse ourselves and go even below his standard of giving?

Page 62

III. The Christian's Gift Should Not Be a Matter of Compulsion (2 Cor. 9: 1-14).

A. *Christians are not ruled by an outward law,* but by an inward Spirit. God's laws for the Christian are not written upon stone or in any book, but upon the heart (Heb. 8:10). The Christian is free in Christ (Rom. 8:2). He has the Bible as a guide in life, and it does contain certain specific commands which he must obey, but there is no elaborate set of statutes covering the details of his life, and he is not bound by law, but set free in the Spirit. He is not bound by outward laws, but motivated by an inward Spirit.

1. Paul is anxious that the church at Corinth make their offering as "a matter of bounty, and not of extortion." The word *extortion* used here has the meaning of *constraint.* Paul wanted them to give freely, and not in any way of compulsion.

2. Notice the terms used in this passage, "not of extortion," "sparingly," "grudgingly or of necessity," "a matter of bounty," "bountifully" and "cheerfully."

3. Our gifts should be from the heart, not as compelled by law. "Let each one as he purposeth in his *heart,* so let him give."

B. *The Lord loves the cheerful giver* and will provide for his needs abundantly.

1. "He will make all grace to abound" to the cheerful giver, "and he will have all sufficiency in all things." He will supply him with seed for sowing, bread for food and increase in the harvest. This is in harmony with the teachings of Jesus (Matt. 6:19-34).

C. *The bountiful and cheerful giver will accomplish at least three things by his giving.*

1. He will "supply the wants of the saints." The "saints" or disciples at Jerusalem and in all Judea were in want because of the famine, and gifts were solicited from the churches abroad to help supply their needs. Paul was solicit-

ing gifts from the church at Corinth for this purpose. One may help today to supply real and keenly felt needs by making contributions to many benevolent causes.

2. He will cause many to "abound with thanksgiving unto God." The true Christian will experience much joy in contributing in any way to that which will glorify God.

3. He will himself be loved and appreciated for his contributions and liberality to those in need.

IV. Examples of Giving Recorded in the New Testament Should Inspire Every Christian to Great Giving.

A. *The members of the church at Jerusalem set us a fine example of giving* (Acts 4:32—5:4).

1. We do not think of the church of Jerusalem as setting an example that we must follow in detail or method, but the same spirit of giving needs to prevail today. Their action was taken under conditions vastly different from our own, and few people will be called upon to make such heroic sacrifices as they made, but the manner in which they met the challenging need of the hour should inspire us to a more heroic self-sacrifice. The fact that "as many as had lands sold them and brought the prices of the things that were sold and laid them at the apostles' feet" should never be forgotten by future generations.

2. No one in that church thought of himself as owner of the things that he possessed. Possession and ownership are two different things and are in no sense identical. One may have possession of a farm, house or business location and still not own it. In the same way we do not own, but only possess, the things we call our own. In truth all things belong to God. "The cattle on a thousand hills are" His (Ps. 50:10).

3. They brought their gifts and "laid them at the apostles' feet." They gave their money without any strings tied to it. Too often today our gifts are conditional.

B. *The churches of Macedonia set a fine example of liberality in giving* (2 Cor. 8:1-5).

1. Paul describes them as being rich in liberality, even though they are in "deep poverty." Liberality can not be truly measured by the amount of money given, but by the spirit with which it is given.

2. They gave "beyond their power," as Paul expresses it. In other words, they gave until it hurt. Too often today it hurts before we have given anything. We need to learn to give, not all that we must, but all that we are able to give to the Lord.

3. They "prayed" Paul to accept their gift. How often we believe today the praying must be from the other person. With them, giving was an opportunity rather than an imposition. Why can't we think of the many worthy and worthwhile missionary and benevolent agencies among us as so many opportunities rather than so many impositions?

4. "They first gave themselves to the Lord." After all, that is the secret of Christian giving. When one truly gives himself to the Lord he will have no difficulty letting loose of a little of his money for the Lord's cause. We need to baptize men's pocketbooks as well as their persons.

C. *The last and greatest example we present, although there are many others that could be given, is Jesus.*

1. Though He was rich He became poor for us (2 Cor. 8:9). "He existed in the form of God . . . yet emptied himself" for man (Phil. 2:6, 7).

2. He not only sacrificed His place in heaven, but He gave away His earthly opportunities. He might have had great earthly possessions. The devil offered Him just such an opportunity in the temptation on the mountain of the wilderness (Matt. 4:8-10). At almost any time during His earthly ministry He might have established a great temporal kingdom and lived in luxury and ease, but He sacrificed it all

and chose to become a wanderer on the earth because of His love for us.

3. He might have enjoyed the pleasures and comforts of an earthly home, but He had no place to lay His head (Matt. 8:20). He went finally to the cross with all its agony and shame, giving His utmost energy and power of endurance for lost man.

GOING ON TO PERFECTION

Introduction: The Christian Life Is a Growth.

A. *Too often we are content to remain babes in Christ.*

1. One cause for this is a false conception of conversion. This false conception assumes that when one is converted he is somehow miraculously endowed with power to remain in a saved condition, hence no further change is necessary, and of course no progress is possible or desirable.

2. There are many others who have been brought to an acceptance of Christ without adequate teaching, who soon fall away and are no longer under the teachings of the church, but who nevertheless have the notion that because they have been baptized they will be saved in the end. These are not concerned about any growth in Christ.

3. There is also the false notion that when we get to heaven we will all receive equal rewards. If we are equal and all receive the same reward, there can be no motive for growth in Christ.

B. *The Christian life is not static or immobile,* but living and progressive.

1. We must not think of ourselves as having reached perfection, but, like Paul, follow after Christ that we may attain greater things (Phil. 3:8-12).

2. We must not be content with what we have done, nor seek to lay again the same foundations, but press for-

ward unto the things that are before (Heb. 6:1; Phil. 3:13).

3. We will not all be rewarded alike, but some will receive greater rewards than others. (a) Some will receive a reward in heaven if they have built an enduring structure upon the foundation of Christ; others will be saved, but receive no reward (1 Cor. 3:10-15). (b) Our works will follow us after death (Rev. 14:13). (c) We will be judged according to our works (Rev. 20:12). These Scriptures and many others indicate that there will be degrees of reward in heaven, and the one who makes the greatest spiritual growth will doubtless produce the greatest works, thus assuring himself of the greatest reward.

4. The Scriptures give us many figures that describe a living, growing, progressive Christian life, a few of which we present in this lesson.

I. The Christian Life Is a Race or Contest.

In this race we should so run that we may attain (1 Cor. 9:24).

A. *The exercise of self-control is essential in the race of life.*

1. In all athletic contests there is a necessity for self-control (1 Cor. 9:25). This is just as true today as it was when Paul penned these words. Those who are masters of themselves and abstain from all forms of dissipation are the surest winners in all contests, and the contest in which we as Christians are engaged is not less difficult and calls for no less of self-control.

2. The truly Christian life is an overcoming life. Notice some of God's promises to him that overcometh:

(a) He will be given to eat of the tree of life (Rev. 2:7).

(b) He shall not suffer hurt of the second death (Rev. 2:11).

(c) He will be given to eat of the hidden manna (Rev. 2:17).

(d) He will be given power over the nations (Rev. 2:26).

(e) He shall be clothed in white raiment (Rev. 3:5).

(f) He will be made a pillar in the temple of God (Rev. 3:12).

(g) He will sit with the Lord (Rev. 3:21).

(h) He will inherit all things (Rev. 21:7).

John tells us that "whosoever is begotten of God overcometh the world" (1 John 5:4), and Paul admonished us to "be not overcome of evil, but overcome evil with good" (Rom. 12:21).

3. Self-control is not something we assume in times of emergency, but an essential quality of the warp and woof of our characters. We will have it when we need it only if we cultivate and build it into our lives. Peter places it among the Christian virtues that go to make up a well-rounded Christian character (2 Pet. 1:6).

B. *In the race of life there is a great goal to be attained.*

1. A great goal is essential to the winning of any contest. Paul had a great goal in view while running the race of life (Phil. 3:14, 15). There was no doubt in his mind as to what he was striving for (1 Cor. 9:26). Abraham had a definite goal in view, "for he looked for a city which hath foundations, whose builder and maker is God" (Heb. 11:8-10), and Moses was able to look beyond the hardships of his condition to an eternal reward (Heb. 11:23-27).

2. The Christian may have the greatest of all possible goals. Athletes strive for a corruptible crown, but we are striving for an incorruptible one (1 Cor. 9:25). Our reward is not temporal glory or material reward, but "an inheritance incorruptible, and undefiled, and that fadeth not away" (1 Pet. 1:4). The Christian's reward is so great that it surpasses anything he has experienced or even imagined (1 Cor. 2:9).

C. *The race of life must be run with patience,* or endurance (Heb. 12:1).

1. Contests are not won by sudden spurts, but by patient endeavor. In the well-known fable of the tortoise and the

hare, the tortoise won, not because it was the swifter, but because it kept right on. It is much the same in the Christian race—many who are capable of doing great things fail because of a lack of stedfast endeavor, while those less gifted win by enduring patience.

2. The members of the first church set an example of stedfastness which we would do well to remember and follow (Acts 2 : 42).

3. After reminding the Corinthians of the coming judgment Paul admonished them to be stedfast in the work of the Lord (1 Cor. 15 : 58).

II. The Christian Life Is the Building of Character (2 Pet. 1: 1-15).

A. *The Lord has made it possible for us to attain a great character.*

1. He has "granted unto us all things that pertain unto life and godliness" (v. 3). In this Christian dispensation we have come into the full inheritance of the promises of God (v. 4). The promise made to Abraham, that in him and his seed should all the nations of the earth be blessed, as well as all the prophecies concerning the coming of Christ and His atoning work, have been fulfilled, and you and I have available a means of salvation.

2. "We have been made partakers of the divine nature" (v. 4). As partakers of divine nature it is possible for us to attain a great character. Having laid such a foundation, we are admonished to "add" or "supply" qualities necessary to the building of a great structure.

B. *He advises us to supply or cultivate seven great qualities.*

1. "In your faith supply virtue," or excellence.

2. "In your virtue knowledge."

3. "In your knowledge self-control."

4. "In your self-control patience," or endurance.

5. "In your patience godliness."

6. "In your godliness brotherly kindness."

7. "And in your brotherly kindness love."

C. *If we build these things into our lives, we will grow great characters.*

1. We will not be idle or unfruitful (v. 8). Jesus condemned the barren fig tree (Matt. 21:18, 19) and declared that we would be His disciples if we bore fruit (John 15:8).

2. We will have great vision, seeing "afar off," but "he that lacketh these things is blind, seeing only what is near" (2 Pet. 1:9).

3. If we do these things, we shall never stumble (2 Pet. 1:10). If we have these things in a perfect degree, we will be perfect, and not only not fail, we will "never stumble." We can not be perfect perhaps, but we will be secure from stumbling to the extent that we have been able to make these things a part of our characters.

4. We will have supplied unto us "an entrance into the eternal kingdom of our Lord and Saviour Jesus Christ (2 Pet. 1:11).

5. These things are of such great importance that we need to be reminded of them constantly. Peter said he would remind his brethren of them always, and provide that after his decease they would still be reminded of them (2 Pet. 1:12-15).

III. The Christian Life Is a Battle (Eph. 6:10-18).

A. *Our battle is not against flesh and blood,* but against great spiritual forces of evil (v. 12).

1. Our battle is "against principalities." The kingdoms of this world are the kingdoms of Satan.

2. Our battle is also "against the powers." There are many powerful organizations working against the best interests of man to which the Christian is necessarily opposed. There are powerful trusts and monopolies, liquor interests and

munitions manufacturers that are often combined, that oppress the people.

3. Our battle is also "against the world rulers of this darkness." All about us—in the business world, in our social contacts, even in the home and school and church—are evil forces. The rulers of darkness seem to be in the ascendency today, and men, women and children are mad and drunk with a licentiousness never known before. Surely we need a great armor in this struggle for righteousness.

B. *Since our battle is against spiritual forces we need a spiritual armor.*

1. This armor must be of God (vs. 10, 11, 13). Man is incapable of defending himself against such an enemy, but must have help from some source greater than himself. He can be strong only "in the strength of the Lord and in the power of his might."

2. We should wear the *whole armor* or strive to make this armor complete. Perfection is the lowest possible divine ideal, and nothing short of a perfect goal should be our aim. We may not be able to reach a perfect state, but we can strive towards it, and the Lord asks always for a whole-hearted endeavor. He requires a complete surrender of life (Matt. 19:16-21; Luke 14:26, 33; Rom. 12:1). He requires the whole tithe (Mal. 3:8-10). He requires a complete obedience (2 Kings 5:1-14; Josh. 6:1-21; Matt. 7:21-27). He requires that we strive towards perfection (Heb. 6:1). Since God has set for us the goal of a whole armor, let us not set our aim any lower than that, but strive to measure up to His standard.

C. *Paul uses the armor of a Roman soldier as an illustration of the Christian's armor* (Eph. 6:14-18).

1. The Christian should have on the girdle of truth. The first great essential in living the Christian life is truthfulness of heart, or integrity of soul. Hypocrisy was severely censured by the Master (Matt. 15:7-9; 23:23-38), and can in no way be of service in fighting the great spiritual battles of life.

Page 72

2. We must have on the breastplate of righteousness. Our lives must be sincere and upright before our fellow men. We must live above the fog of petty scheming and unrighteous dealings if our characters are to withstand the assaults of Satan.

3. Our feet must "be shod with the preparation of the gospel of peace." The feet and the gospel are connected elsewhere in the Scriptures (Isa. 52:7; Nah. 1:15; Rom. 10:15), which indicates that the gospel is to be carried to the ends of the earth. It should be the supreme desire of every Christian to help carry this message of glad tidings, either in person or by proxy, to the peoples of all the earth.

4. The shield of faith must be a part of this armor. The one who lacks faith is terribly handicapped in the battle against the spiritual wickedness of the world, but with faith great things are accomplished. Witness the heroes of the Bible as recorded in the eleventh chapter of Hebrews.

5. We must also have the helmet of salvation. When one is assured of salvation he can fight in any battle. Men may kill his body, but his soul is secure.

6. The Sword of the Spirit, or Word of God, is a part of this armor. Every Christian should be sufficiently acquainted with the Word to be able to use it effectively in fighting personal sins in his own life, and eliminating sin from the lives of others. With it he may cut both ways, dividing between right and wrong in his own life and in the lives of his fellow men (Heb. 4:12).

7. Finally, as soldiers, we must keep in touch with God through prayer. All our equipment for the battle of life will not enable us to fight successfully unless we can enlist His help in prayer.

THE DANGER OF APOSTASY

Introduction: **The Danger of Apostasy Is Not Imaginary, But Real.**

A. *This is a much neglected subject.* We have done much to bring men to Christ, but we have been almost sinfully neglectful of them afterwards, and in thousands of cases they have been allowed to "shrink back unto perdition" (Heb. 10: 38, 39).

1. In every church there are more who are not active in the church than there are those that are, and some of these have gone completely back into the world. Some of these were elders and deacons, Bible-school superintendents and teachers, musicians and heads of various organized activities, and have now become of less than no value to Christ and His church.

2. Some whose names are on church books, who at one time openly avowed themselves as servants of Christ, who were touched by the story of the matchless love and sacrifice of Christ, and who began with high resolve to follow Him, now even openly declare themselves as opposed to Christ and the church.

3. This lesson is, therefore, not an attempt to merely add another lesson to a course of instructions, but an attempt to supply a much needed teaching upon a greatly neglected subject.

Page 74

I. According to the Scriptures, There Is a State or Condition of Life that Is Worse than That of One Who Has Never Accepted Christ.

A. *It is possible for one to be lost after he has been saved.*

1. The doctrine of "Once in grace, always in grace" is a false doctrine, for one may fall from grace (Gal. 5:4). In this passage Paul declared that the Jews who had been converted to Christ, but afterwards insisted on circumcision, had severed themselves from Christ and fallen from grace. If it were possible for the Jews to fall from grace because they insisted upon living under the law, it is also possible for others to fall from grace who refuse to live under the law of Christ.

2. It is possible for the best of Christians to fall away and finally be rejected. The apostle Paul, whose life after his conversion was above reproach, feared that after he had preached to others he might himself be rejected (1 Cor. 9:27). If Paul was not exempt from this danger, who of us dare claim exemption?

B. *Paul follows the statement of his own fears of being rejected* by citing several groups of the Old Testament which were once God's chosen people, but were rejected because of their willful and deliberate sins (1 Cor. 10:1-10).

1. He first mentions those who became idolaters, who made the golden calf, and three thousand of them fell in one day. In spite of their wonderful deliverance from a terrible condition of slavery, they repudiated the God who had delivered them and turned back to the practices of the very Egyptians who had oppressed them (1 Cor. 10:7; Ex. 32:1-35).

2. He next mentions the twenty-three thousand who committed fornication and fell in one day. These who had but recently received the law had broken that law in at least two points—they had committed fornication and turned back to idolatry. They had been God's chosen people, but they fell from grace by their deliberate disobedience.

3. He refers again to the children of Israel who tempted the Lord with their unreasonable complainings and called in question His very existence, and that after having personally received His especial favor and blessing. Of these many were destroyed by serpents (1 Cor. 10:9; Num. 21:4-6).

4. The fourth and last group mentioned are those who murmured against Him at Kadesh, including all but Caleb and Joshua, and were condemned to die in the wilderness without ever entering the promised land (1 Cor. 10:10; Num. 14:1-37).

Here are four groups, all of them God's select and chosen people, who fell from their favored position and were rejected by the Lord because of their willful disobedience, and the warning, based upon these examples of waywardness, is, "Let him that thinketh he standeth take heed lest he fall" (1 Cor. 10:12).

II. Willful Sinning Leads to a State or Condition of Complete Apostasy in Which One Blasphemes the Holy Spirit.

A. *God will pardon any and all who sincerely seek His pardon.* Note the following declarations of Scripture:

1. "Though your sins be as scarlet, they shall be as white as snow; though they be red like crimson, they shall be as wool" (Isa. 1:18).

2. "He will abundantly pardon" the wicked and unrighteous who return to Him (Isa. 55:6, 7).

3. He forgives *all* our iniquities (Ps. 103:3).

4. "*All manner* of sin and blaspheming shall be forgiven unto men" (Matt. 12:31, K. J.).

5. "He that will, let him take of the water of life freely" (Rev. 22:17).

6. The "sin unto death" in 1 John 5:16, 17 is not a specific sin, but a condition of heart and life. In the marginal references of many Standard Revised Bibles the term "a sin"

is rendered simply "sin." Thus it is not *a sin* in particular, but simply *sin* in general, that John is writing about.

7. The references in Matt. 12:32 and Luke 12:10 say, "Whosoever *speaketh a word* against the Son of man," but "Whosoever *speaketh* against the Holy Spirit." Jesus was not talking about the speaking of one specific word, either about the Son of man or the Holy Spirit for that matter, but about a more general speech or conversation. He was talking about blaspheming, ridiculing and repudiating the Holy Spirit.

B. *To blaspheme the Holy Spirit is to lightly esteem, ridicule and repudiate the work of redemption* previously wrought in our lives through the agency of the Holy Spirit.

1. Those who have never been redeemed can not reach this condition, because they have never received the Holy Spirit nor enjoyed the experience of salvation.

2. In Matthew 12 Jesus was speaking to a group who, while they could not possibly blaspheme the Holy Spirit, because they lived before the Spirit was given and before one could experience a New Testament conversion, yet they had employed the same principle in their denial of Christ's sonship. Jesus had wrought many miracles that were incontestible and that established His sonship in the minds of all fair-minded people, and he was daily fulfilling their own Scriptures, and in spite of their knowledge of these things they were willfully and deliberately rejecting Him as the promised Messiah. Jesus is pointing to the fact that those in the following dispensation who, having experienced the love of God and the power of the Holy Spirit, shall then lightly esteem and ridicule these things, shall not be able to receive forgiveness. Thus He intimates to them that they are themselves in danger of the displeasure of God because of their unfair, insincere and stubborn attitude (Matt. 12:22-42).

C. *The last state may be worse than the first.* One may reach a state worse than that of never having become a Christian. There is a chance for any one who has not become a Christian, for at any time he may accept Christ, but there is not a chance for one who has, after becoming a Christian, turned his back upon these things completely, in absolute apostasy.

1. Peter gives warning against just such a condition as this (2 Pet. 2: 20-22). He refers to those who have become Christians, who "have escaped the defilements of the world through the knowledge of the Lord and Saviour Jesus Christ" and have "known the way of righteousness." If these are "again entangled" and overcome, the latter end is worse than the first. They are as bad off as "the dog that has returned to his own vomit" (how repulsive!), or the "sow that was washed to her wallowing in the mire" (how dumb!).

2. Jesus must have had this same condition in mind when He gave the parable of the unclean spirits (Matt. 12: 43-45).

D. *We may even reach an impossible state, or a condition of heart wherein it will be impossible for us to return to the Lord* (Heb. 6: 4-6).

1. The reference here in Hebrews, like that in 2 Peter, is to those who have been converted and become children of God; to "those who were once enlightened and tasted of the heavenly gift, and were made partakers of the Holy Spirit, and tasted the good word of God, and the powers of the age to come." When such fall away they can not be brought back to repentance, because "they crucify to themselves the Son of God afresh and hold him up to an open shame." In this connection the writer employs the strong word "impossible," which places the one who has thus fallen away in a position which is not at all to be desired. Let us be very careful that we do not reach that impossible state.

2. Men may reach a state where God will give them up. Those of whom Paul was writing in the first chapter of the Roman letter were so reprobate that three times (vs. 24, 26 and 28) it is said that "God gave them up."

3. When men sin, or rather live in a state of sin, willfully, "there remaineth no more a sacrifice for sin" (Heb. 10:26). When one has once come under the sway of the story of a crucified Lord, and then deliberately turns away from Him, every means for his salvation has been exhausted and there is nothing more that can be done for him. He is therefore lost. There is no story greater than the story of the cross, and God has appointed no other means of salvation. The one who has turned away in spite of all this will not come back to God, and God can not save him unless he does. This does not mean, however, that every Christian who sins, or for a time goes astray, can not again be brought back to God and find forgiveness, for as Christians we have the blessed privilege of coming back to Him at any time. "If we confess our sins, he is faithful and righteous to forgive us our sins, and to cleanse us from all unrighteousness" (1 John 1:9). But he who habitually lives in a state of willful sin may be out of reach even of the wonderful mercy and love of God. In this sense he is in a worse condition than one who has never been saved.

III. To Fail in Our Regular Attendance Upon the Services of the Lord's House Is to Court the Danger of Complete Apostasy (Heb. 10:19-31).

A. *We need to constantly draw near to God* (vs. 19-23). Too often we "follow him afar off." We miss the warmth and glow of close communion and fellowship with the heavenly Father, and are easily led into sin, which in turn may lead us into complete apostasy.

1. We may now enter boldly into the holy place by the blood of Jesus (vs. 19-21), and here we may receive help in meeting the temptations of life. A life that is hid with Christ in God is in no danger of apostasy.

2. We are invited to come with pure hearts, and yet without fear, to the throne of grace (v. 22). What a blessed

privilege to thus with assurance and confidence approach His throne!

3. We are warned to "hold fast . . . without wavering" (v. 23). When we forget the place of prayer we are in danger of letting go of our faith.

B. *If we assemble with God's people regularly, we will be in less danger of apostasy.*

1. We should assemble to "provoke one another to love and good works" (v. 24). We grow by association. The fellowship of the church supplies a distinct need in our lives and "provokes" us to greater endeavor. When we are working for Jesus we are not in much danger of going into a state of apostasy.

2. We should assemble ourselves together because the day is drawing near (v. 25). If there were no judgment, we might well cease to attend church, but in view of the coming day there is danger in doing so.

3. Failure to assemble habitually may be, and probably most often is, deliberate and willful sin, and deliberate and willful sin may lead us into complete apostasy, from which there is no redemption (v. 26). The Lord has, at great cost to Himself, provided the place of assembly for our edification. This is His plan and purpose; to turn our backs and deliberately refuse the Lord's Table and the preaching of His Word is to violate His will and destroy the bond that ties us to Him. Each time we remain away from church makes it easier to remain away again, and to remain away habitually lays us open to all the temptations of the world, and complete and final apostasy is the natural result of such a course.

C. *Those who thus willfully become apostate may look forward only to the sorest punishment in the day of judgment.*

1. For them the only sacrifice for sin—that of Christ upon the cross—has not been sufficient, and there is no more (v. 26); and their only prospect is that of a fearful judgment which shall consume all the foes of God (v. 27). In thus turning

away from God we have become His foes and will be destroyed with His adversaries.

2. The judgment reserved for those who, having once tasted of all the good things of God in full salvation from sin, turn their backs upon it all and repudiate the faith they once held, is not at all pleasant to contemplate. The man who despised Moses' law died without mercy, but he who despises the sacrificing love of Christ, "who hath trodden under foot the Son of God, and hath counted the blood of the covenant wherewith he was sanctified an unholy thing, and hath done despite unto the Spirit of grace," deserves only the wrath of God. And the wrath of God will be no quiet sinking into oblivion, for "we know him who said, Vengeance belongeth unto me, I will recompense. And again, The Lord shall judge his people. It is a fearful thing to fall into the hands of the living God" (vs. 26-31).

D. *And this day of judgment is drawing near,* therefore we have need of patience or stedfastness (vs. 36-39).

1. Stedfastness is a quality that is a necessity in living the Christian life, as we have seen in Lesson 10. We must have stedfastness in church attendance and stedfastness in Christian living, for without this we will not receive the promise of God (v. 36).

2. In "a very little while" He will come (v. 37). The Scriptures teach that the second coming of Christ is imminent. Hosea's prophecy was recorded about six hundred years before Christ, and the Book of Hebrews was written nearly two thousand years ago, but they refer to the coming of Christ as something that could not be far off and might be expected any moment, or in "a very little while." And they were not mistaken about it as some think. To us two thousand years is a long time, but "one day is with the Lord as a thousand years, and a thousand years as one day" (2 Pet. 3:8). The time in any case will be short for us. If He comes during our lifetime, it can not be far off, for life is short at best.

And after we are dead we have passed into eternity, where time does not exist; with us, as with the Lord, one day may then be as a thousand years, and a thousand years may be only as a day.

3. Let us be, then, "not of them that shrink back unto perdition; but of them that have faith unto the saving of the soul" (Heb. 10: 38, 39). Let us be stedfast in our attendance at the services of the Lord's house; let us not deny the Christ in our daily lives, and let us not forget the imminence of His second coming, but by stedfast loyalty prepare to meet Him when He comes.

NOTE.—Heb. 12: 12-29 should also be read in connection with this lesson.

A BRIEF, CONDENSED HISTORY OF THE RESTORATION MOVEMENT

I. Causes of Division and Seeds of Denominationalism.

A. *Imperfections in the church cause divisions.*

1. The church is not, and never has been, a perfect institution. She has her human as well as her divine side, and not until "this mortal shall have put on immortality" will she be perfect. It is true that the church as set up by the apostles was a perfect pattern, but the human element in her was imperfect even from the beginning. Even during the lifetime of the apostlès these imperfect human elements began to show in the church.

(a) The light from the cloven tongues of Pentecost had scarcely ceased to glow when Ananias and Sapphira attempted to deceive the Holy Spirit and were disciplined by death, and the Grecian widows were neglected in the daily ministrations (Acts 4: 32—5: 10; 6: 1-6).

2. Factions and divisions began to arise during the days of the apostles.

(a) At Corinth there were four parties claiming as many different names (1 Cor. 1: 10-13; 3: 1-10).

(b) It is also evident from Paul's letter to the Ephesians that there were disturbances there that might lead to divisions, if there were not actual divisions there (Eph. 4: 1-6).

(c) At Antioch and elsewhere Jews, converted to Christianity, created disturbing factions (Acts 15:1-32). Read also the Books of Romans and Galatians.

3. Inspired apostles prophesied a falling away from the faith (2 Thess. 2:1-12; Acts 20:29, 30; 1 Tim. 4:1-3; 2 Tim. 3:1-9).

With the above facts in mind we should not be unprepared to find that the church, after the death of all the apostles, is led into a state of apostasy and division.

B. *The rise of papal power kept the people in darkness and ignorance of the Bible,* and a number of abuses came gradually into the life of the church. We shall attempt to enumerate a few of these abuses here:

1. One of the first of these was the perversion of the office of elder. The elder in the New Testament church had only the authority of a shepherd, or overseer, but in time he came to assume powers that were not Scripturally his, and became the virtual head of the local congregation. Then the leading elder in a group of churches came to be head over the group, and this brought about the "bishop," who had an office distinct from and superior to that of the elder. Later power and authority was further concentrated into the hands of patriarchs who had authority over the bishops. In A. D. 460, Pope Leo I claimed authority over the patriarchs, and about a century later the patriarch at Constantinople tried to assume the rank of "universal bishop," but failed. In A. D. 590, Pope Leo III was invested with temporal powers and recognized as the head of the whole church by Charlemagne, and in A. D. 1870 the Vatican Council decreed that the pope, speaking *ex cathedra*, or as the head of the church, was the voice of God, and therefore infallible. Thus by gradual stages the simple office of the elder of the New Testament church became the perverted and exalted office of the pope of Rome.

2. The invention of purgatory, which was supposed to be some kind of place of punishment beyond the grave from

Page 84

which one could be extricated by living relatives or friends, and the selling of indulgences which instituted a system of extortion surpassing anything of its kind in history, further corrupted the purity and simplicity of the church and contributed to the decay and ultimate divisions in the body of Christ.

3. The name and ordinances of the church were changed from their apostolic simplicity and purity. Instead of "church of Christ" of the New Testament, the name "Holy Roman Catholic Church" was substituted. Instead of the simple and yet beautiful ordinances of the Lord's Supper and Christian immersion, a complicated theory of the Lord's Supper, which it was difficult to understand, and sprinkling and pouring for baptism, were introduced.

4. Doubtless the factor that contributed most to the divided state of succeeding Protestantism was the suppression of the reading of the Bible by the people. The Bible became a closed Book. The priests claimed to be its sole interpreters, and the people were left in ignorance of its teachings. The translation of the Bible into the English language, that many more might read, was bitterly opposed by the Roman Church, and many men suffered persecutions and even death in their attempts to translate it.

C. *The beginning of the Protestant Reformation may be said to mark the rise of denominationalism.*

1. The reformation was born in an atmosphere surcharged with general ignorance of the Bible, priestly abuses and a widespread discontent among the people. While it is impossible to set exact dates, we may safely say that it began with the fourteenth century and extended into the fifteenth with increasing vigor and acceptance. (a) John Wycliffe (1320-1384) was the "morning star of the Reformation," appearing in the dark hour just before the dawn. His greatest contribution was the translation of the Bible into the English language for the first time. (b) John Huss, a native of Ger-

many, influenced by the writings of Wycliffe, preached the Scriptures in opposition to the false teachings of the Roman Church, and paid for his consecration and loyalty with his life at the stake. (c) Girolamo Savonarola (1452-1498), an outspoken Italian priest residing in Florence, boldly condemned the evils of the Roman Church and even of the pope. He was burned at the stake on May 23, 1498. (d) Martin Luther, recognized by all Protestants as the leading spirit of the Reformation, translated the Bible into the German language, defied the pope and the whole Roman Church, opposed the sale of indulgences, taught the Scriptural doctrine of the priesthood of all believers and gave the opened Bible to all the world. (e) There were many others who were important factors in the Reformation whose names only we will take space to mention here: Erasmus, Melanchthon, Zwingli, John Calvin, John Knox and John and Charles Wesley.

2. The personalities of great men led to denominationalism. When we have a great man with a great message he is likely to have a great following. And the next step is an easy and natural one, for such followings, imbued with religious zeal and idealism, have a tendency to crystallize into a denomination. Thus it was in the days of the Reformation and afterwards. Martin Luther was a great man with a great message, and his followers, numbering into the thousands, have become a great denomination. John Knox was a great reformer and the father of Presbyterianism; John Wesley was a consecrated and devout soul with a great message, and the Methodist denomination is the result. So that at least one of the major causes of denominationalism may be said to be following men in a sort of hero worship, rather than following the Christ who alone is worthy of worship. By so doing, men have built fences and separated the people of God.

3. Another important factor in bringing about a divided church was the writing of creeds. (a) In the year of 1530, when the Roman Church called a diet in the city of Augs-

burg in an effort to compel the Protestants to yield to the claims of Roman authority, Melanchthon, the friend of Luther and a brilliant reformer, drew up what is known as the Augsburg Confession of Faith, and influenced the diet to adopt it. (b) In 1552, Bishop Cranmer prepared a creed by the order of King Henry VIII, which was adopted by the Episcopal Church. (c) Many other creeds have been written and adopted by church bodies since those days, further separating the people of God and establishing denominational fences.

II. The Beginning of the Restoration Movement.

A. *At the beginning of the nineteenth century there arose a spontaneous and simultaneous movement which had as its objective the restoration of the teachings and practices of the New Testament church.*

1. Back of the Restoration movement in America in the nineteenth century, however, are some important roots in the Old World that should not be overlooked. There was a church of Christ at Morrison's Court, Glasgow, in 1778; there was a church of Christ at Leith Walk, Edinburgh, in 1798; the church at Criccieth, North Wales, was in existence in 1795; there was a church of the New Testament order at Tubemore, Ireland, in 1807, and there was a church of Christ at Manchester and one at Dublin, in 1810.

B. *In America there arose in various places at about the same time leaders who advocated a return to the simple teachings of the Bible.* Tired of denominationalism with its bickerings and fightings, its human creeds and beclouded theology, its departure from and misuse of the Scriptures, they sought a way out by a careful study and diligent application of the will of God as revealed in the New Testament.

1. A short time after the close of the Revolutionary War, James O'Kelly, a prominent Methodist minister of Virginia, but who was at that time preaching in the Carolinas, having

been a soldier in the war and imbibed the democratic ideals of the times, vigorously opposed the re-establishment of the authority of bishops and led in a revolt against Asbury, who had been appointed bishop by Wesley. The controversy came to a head at a conference held at Baltimore in 1793. O'Kelly and his following lost in the fight for a democratic decision and a great number of them pulled away from the Methodist Episcopal Church. The new movement adopted the name ''Christians simply,'' and took the Bible alone as their creed. It is estimated that the Methodist Church sustained a loss of from seven to nine thousand members as a result of this secession, and the new movement spread rapidly, especially in Virginia and North Carolina.

2. In 1800, Dr. Abner Jones, a Baptist physician of Hartford, Conn., and Elias Smith, another prominent Baptist, tiring of human creeds, urged that such things be abandoned and that the people return to the simplicity of the New Testament. In September, 1802, they organized a church of twenty-five members at Lyndon, Vt. The same year churches were also organized at Hanover and Bradford, N. H., and in March, 1803, a church was formed at Piermont, N. H. Within a few years the new party had organized churches in the New England States, New York, New Jersey and Pennsylvania.

3. In 1810, John Wright, a Free Baptist, organized a Free Baptist Church which recognized no articles of faith as authoritative. In 1813, under the leadership of Wright, an Association of Free Baptists was formed. This association soon dropped the name Baptist and declared that the Bible, ''without note or comment,'' was their only creed. This movement grew until in 1820 these churches rivaled the Methodist in numbers in Indiana.

4. The largest and one of the most important of these movements was that led by Barton W. Stone, a prominent and powerful preacher of Kentucky. Stone was reared in the Presbyterian faith, but early began to disagree with some

of the teachings of the Presbyterian Church, and was ordained to the ministry by the Presbyterian Synod with reservations. In 1801 he led in a revival at Cane Ridge, Ky., which was one of the most famed in American history. Great crowds came on foot, in wagons and on horseback, and remained until the food supply of the countryside was exhausted. Nearly three thousand were in attendance at one time. Stone, with four other preachers, was suspended from the Presbyterian Church for preaching against the doctrines of Calvinism and the Presbyterian Confession of Faith, and they immediately constituted themselves into what they at first called ''The Springfield Presbytery.'' The ''Apology of the Springfield Presbytery,'' in which they denounced authoritative confessions of faith and creeds, and proclaimed the Bible as their only rule of faith and practice, was then published by them. In less than a year after forming the Springfield Presbytery they decided that their name savored too much of denominationalism and ''threw it overboard and took the name Christian.'' Their work had far-reaching results, and in a short time churches were established in many places. In a few years this group numbered into the thousands.

5. In western Pennsylvania there arose a movement out of which there was destined to come a leader who would unite all these groups into one and steer the new ship through many troubled waters. In the year of 1807, Thomas Campbell, a Seceder Presbyterian preacher from Ireland, was assigned to a church near Pittsburgh. Mr. Campbell was a man of splendid education, having attended Glasgow University in the Old World and graduated with honors, and he had a great zeal for uniting the broken factions of the church. Before leaving Ireland for America he had attempted to bring together the warring elements in the Presbyterian Church there, and his burning zeal for this cause was not cooled by his failure to accomplish unity there, or his removal to America. Soon after taking up his duties as pastor in Pennsylvania he was dis-

ciplined by the Presbytery for admitting others than Seceder Presbyterians to the communion. Reluctantly he withdrew from the association, and, with his followers, formed "The Christian Association of Washington, Pa." He was commissioned by this group to write a declaration of its aims. In compliance with this commission he produced a document, known as the "Declaration and Address," which has become historic. In the address he set forth the position of the association in denouncing creeds and separating themselves from denominational authority.

(a) When the Declaration and Address was just coming off the press in 1809, his son Alexander arrived. While the Restoration movement is not a Campbellite movement, Alexander Campbell is recognized by all as the greatest of all its leaders. As an author and editor he stands in the first rank; as an educator, Bethany College stands as a monument today; as a debater, he was never vanquished; as a preacher, he attracted and held spellbound great multitudes, and, as a religious leader, he gathered about him a host of talented and consecrated men and women whose influence will be felt and recognized many years hence.

(b) Strange as it may seem, father and son, separated by thousands of miles of ocean, had come to the same conclusions in their study of the religious problems of the day and could go happily on together.

(c) Unwilling to create another sect in an already divided church, Thomas Campbell, on Oct. 4, 1810, applied to Pittsburgh Synod of the Presbyterian Church for admission, but was refused. Against his wishes he was then forced to organize the "Christian Association," already mentioned, into a church. In May, 1811, this was done, and they were known as "The Brush Run Church." Soon after this, upon a careful study of the Scriptures, they accepted immersion as the only Scriptural baptism, and, together with a number of others, were immersed in July, 1812.

Page 90

C. By A. D. 1835 the cause had made substantial growth, and the forces were co-operating over a wide area.

1. Their acceptance of immersion as baptism gave the Restorationists favor with the Baptists, and in 1813 they were invited to join the Redstone Baptist Association, which they did. Alexander Campbell soon became the leader of the movement and was a popular speaker with his Baptist friends. He was ably assisted in the work by a number of powerful preachers. Among these were Walter Scott, "Raccoon" John Smith, P. S. Fall, the Creaths, Vardman, John T. Johnson, William Hodges, Adamson Bently, Joseph Gaston and others. On Aug. 30, 1816, Mr. Campbell preached a sermon on the law to the Redstone Baptist Association, which became the entering wedge that finally separated the two groups. When compelled to leave the Redstone Association they went to the Mahoning Baptist Association, but in 1830 they had been rejected by the Mahoning association and practically all other Baptist associations, and were compelled to seek a separate organization. They then came to be known as "Christians" or "Disciples of Christ," and their churches were known as "Christian Churches" or "Churches of Christ."

2. In 1832 there was at Lexington, Ky., a fusion of the forces of the Campbells numbering about twelve thousand with those of Stone, which comprised about fifteen thousand members. In Ohio, Walter Scott and Joseph Gaston joined forces, preaching in Baptist and Christian Connection churches, and in Indiana, Mathes and Wright had joined fellowship in the Christian Connection and Reformed groups. Thus the work of union and fusion went on until by the year of 1835 the forces were well united in a common cause.

3. The subsequent history of the Restoration movement is the story of successes and failures, battles and love feasts, disappointments and glorious victories, but withal the story of great achievements by brave-hearted and loyal followers of the Christ of Galilee.

For the benefit of the pupil who wishes to investigate the accuracy of the statements made above, or to gain a fuller and more comprehensive understanding of this subject, we list here a few of the many books that have been consulted:

"Popular Outline of Church History," by Frederick J. Gielow; "Adventuring Towards Christian Unity," by Dean Walker; "Concerning the Disciples," by P. H. Welshimer; "Origin and Early History of the Disciples of Christ," by Walter W. Jennings; "How the Disciples Began and Grew," by M. M. Davis; "The Disciples," by B. A. Abbott, and the "Cane Ridge Meetinghouse," by James R. Rogers.

THE PRINCIPLES OF THE RESTORATION MOVEMENT

I. The Parent Stem.

The principles of the Restoration movement may be said to have all grown out of one parent stem; i. e., the acceptance of the Bible as an only rule of faith and practice.

A. *This was the principle first announced by the leaders of the movement in various sections.*

1. James O'Kelly and his brethren in Virginia early adopted the principle of taking "the Bible itself as their only creed" ("Origin and Early History of the Disciples of Christ," pp. 55-63).

2. Dr. Abner Jones in Vermont and New Hampshire secured a great following among the Baptists. He taught that we should reject human names and creeds and have "no name but Christian, and no law but the Bible" (" How the Disciples Began and Grew," p. 23).

3. The many congregations established around the movement led by Barton W. Stone would accept no book of discipline but the Bible ("How the Disciples Began and Grew," pp. 23, 24; "The Cane Ridge Meetinghouse," pp. 172-177).

4. The movement, as led by Thomas and Alexander Campbell, was built largely upon the principle that the Bible was the only rule and guide in the conduct of the affairs of the church. The famous slogan of Thomas Campbell, "Where the

Scriptures speak we speak, and where the Scriptures are silent we are silent''; his Declaration and Address, as well as all the subsequent writings of that great leader, Alexander Campbell, ring with the message and sound forth the clarion call of complete submission to, and dependence upon the Bible as an all-sufficient rule of faith and practice (''How the Disciples Began and Grew,'' pp. 46-48, 53-63).

B. *The adoption of this fundamental principle was doubtless induced by many causes,* only a few of which we have space to mention here:

1. There was the arrogant and intolerant spirit of bishops and synods.

(a) James O'Kelly objected and protested against the re-establishment and strengthening of the Methodist Episcopate (''Origin and Early History of the Disciples of Christ,'' pp. 55-60).

(b) Thomas Campbell could not agree with the Presbytery in the matter of the communion, and was compelled to leave that body (''How the Disciples Began and Grew,'' pp. 43-46).

(c) Barton W. Stone and his colaborers were compelled against their wishes to withdraw from the Presbytery because they dared preach against the un-Scriptural teachings and practices of that body, and the persecutions instituted against them were bitter, unjust and manifestly un-Christian (''Cane Ridge Meetinghouse,'' pp. 165-171).

2. The desire for Christian unity was a contributing factor in bringing about the adoption of the Bible as a rule of faith and practice. The churches were woefully divided, and bitter hatreds, jealousies and rivalries existed between the churches of that day. Thomas Campbell had a great passion for the unity of God's people, even antedating his coming to America, and Barton W. Stone was fired with a holy zeal for the same cause.

So prominent was this factor that many have, incorrectly, we think, assumed that the desire for Christian unity was the very genius of the movement. But a more careful analysis will discover the fact that, while Christian unity was a prominent contributing factor in the beginning, and has continued to hold a prominent place in our preaching, the acceptance of the Bible alone as a rule of faith and practice has been the guiding star of the Restoration movement.

II. The Adoption of This Principle Naturally Led to a More Careful Study and Analysis of the Scriptures, and Out of This Diligent Study Came the Teaching of Great Bible Truths or Principles.

A. *One of the most important of these principles was the restoration of the church of the New Testament in all of its essentials.*

1. It was from this principle that the movement took its name, and it was the achievement of this purpose to which the movement was primarily devoted.

2. The movement was not a *reformation,* but a *restoration.* Tired of the denominationalism of the day, with its bigotry and warring factions, the leaders of this movement sought to go back of all denominational systems to the fountain head as the source of all their teachings and practices. They went back of denominationalism, back of Protestantism, back of Roman Catholicism even, and discovered the church of Christ and the apostles, and proclaimed it as the only safe pattern for men to follow in restoring the church of Christ.

3. The adoption of this principle did not involve the finding of an exact and detailed pattern of the church with a set of laws that should govern the church in every particular item, for it was only in the great essentials of the gospel that the church was to be restored. Among these essentials they sought to restore were the following:

(a) The name. They believed in calling Bible things by Bible names to avoid confusion of thought. They also saw in denominational names a cause of division and a failure to glorify God. They were not averse to using any of the many Bible designations for the followers of Christ, such as Christians, disciples, saints, brethren, etc., but the name by which they finally came to be known most was Christians or Disciples.

(b) The ordinances of the church. While the ordinances of the church were being observed by the denominations they were not being Scripturally observed.

(1) The Lord's Supper was surrounded by a multitude of false teachings and practices, such as "close communion," "feet washing," and the peculiar and fantastic teachings of the Roman Catholic Church. Protestant bodies were also failing to observe it every Lord's Day, as the Scriptures indicated. The fathers of the Restoration sought to restore it to its proper weekly observance as a simple memorial of the death of Christ on the cross.

(2) Immersion, which is the only baptism recognized in the New Testament, had been replaced by sprinkling and pouring as the almost universal practice of the churches, and they sought to restore the original practice of immersion.

(c) The conditions of salvation. Among the false teachings concerning this subject in that day was Calvinism, which taught that man was powerless to help himself, and that he must wait for God to save him, and the notion that man must have some kind of a miraculous experience (the more miraculous the better) before he could be saved or accepted into the church. The leaders of the Restoration movement pointed out the simple plan of the New Testament, and multitudes accepted Christ in this way. Their simple New Testament plan involved only:

1. Faith in Christ as the Son of God (Matt. 16:16; Mark 8:29).

2. Repentance for past sins (Luke 24:46, 47; Acts 2:38; 3:19).

3. An open confession of Christ before men (Matt. 10:32, 33; Rom. 10:9, 10).

4. And immersion in water in obedience to His commands (Matt. 28:19, 20; Acts 2:38).

B. *Another important principle stressed by the Restoration movement was a proper distinction between the old and the new covenants.*

1. In an epoch-making "Sermon on the Law," Alexander Campbell pointed out for the first time this distinction. As M. M. Davis says, he showed that "the law was temporary and local, but the gospel was for all time and universal. The type had given way to the antitype, the shadow to the substance. As a system the law had waxed old and passed away. Only the ethical, which was necessarily immortal, remained. The patriarchal dispensation was the starlight; the Jewish dispensation, the moonlight; that of John the Baptist was the twilight, and the Christian dispensation . . . was the full sunlight" age.

2. This clear distinction between the law and the gospel, or between the old and the new covenants, proved an impregnable bulwark to Mr. Campbell in subsequent debates and discussions, and gave to the Restoration preachers a mighty weapon in combating the evils of denominationalism in the years that followed.

3. A knowledge of this distinction is an essential in the understanding of the Bible on the part of those who read and teach it today. For this reason we would counsel a careful reading and study of the following Scriptural teaching on the subject:

(a) The law was called a copy, shadow and pattern of heavenly things (Heb. 8:5).

(b) The law is said to have been faulty (Heb. 8:7, 8).

(c) It is said to have been aged and near vanishing (Heb. 8:13).

(d) It is said to have been passing away (2 Cor. 3:7)

(e) It is said to have been done away in Christ (2 Cor. 3:14).

(f) It is said to have been blotted out, taken out of the way and nailed to His cross (Col. 2:14).

(g) A new covenant was promised to the people of God (Jer. 31:31-34; Heb. 8:8-12).

(h) This new covenant was dedicated in the blood of Jesus (Luke 22:20; Heb. 9:11-28).

(i) This new covenant was to be opened by the apostles (Matt. 16:17-19).

(j) This new covenant was to be effective only after the death of Christ (Heb. 9:16, 17).

(k) This new covenant was to be an everlasting covenant (Heb. 13:21).

C. *The autonomy of the local church was another great principle of this movement.*

1. The denominational churches had built up great ecclesiastical systems that controlled the churches, and were many times arrogant and oppressive in their dealings with the churches.

2. The Revolutionary War and the principles for which the American pioneers fought were still fresh in the minds of the people at the beginning of the Restoration movement. The spirit of freedom and democracy prevailed everywhere. It is little wonder then that a new religious movement, planted in the warm soil of America's new-found freedom, should declare for democracy in the church.

3. Moreover, a careful reading of the Scriptures confirmed this same democratic view.

(a) They found that the New Testament church had only a local organization, and that even the mother church at Jerusalem, where the apostles held membership, was only advisory in its power (Acts 15:1-33).

(b) They found that, instead of an elder or bishop having charge of a plurality of churches, there was a plurality of elders in each church (Acts 11:29, 30; 14:23; 15:2-4; Tit. 1:5; Jas. 5:14).

Page 98

(c) They found that the organization of the New Testa ment church was a simple one, composed only of elders and deacons, and not a great ecclesiastical machine (Acts 6:1-6; 1 Tim. 3:1-16).

Hence the early leaders of the Restoration movement renounced the authority of Presbyteries and Synods, and refused to be bound by any kind of ecclesiastical authority or ruling whatsoever.

D. *Yet another important principle of the Restoration movement was the recognition and exaltation of Christ as the "head over all things to the church."*

1. The matter of authority has always been a troublesome one. It was the assumption of undue authority, as we have already seen in a former chapter, that led to the rise of the papacy and brought upon us the Dark Ages. In the beginning of the Restoration movement, much the same as today, important authority was vested in the church. With the Roman Catholic Church, supreme authority was accorded the pope of Rome; in the Methodist Church the bishop had considerable authority; in the Presbyterian Church important authority was assumed by the Synod or Presbytery, and in the Baptist Churches the local congregations dared to exercise authority concerning the fitness of candidates for baptism, or their participation in the Lord's Supper.

2. The pioneers of the Restoration believed and taught that, as Thomas Campbell said in the Declaration and Address, the ordinances of the church must rest entirely in the authority of Christ, and that no one has a right to add to or take from the Word in regard to them. They also denied the authority of the creeds, and held themselves amenable only to Christ in religious matters.

3. A careful search of the Scriptures revealed that Christ had claimed "all authority, both in heaven and on earth" (Matt. 28:18), and that He was "head over all things to the church" (Eph. 1:22; 5:23; Col. 1:18).

E. *Christian unity, while not the main issue of the Restoration movement, became an abiding principle of it.*

1. Thomas Campbell had said, "The church of Christ on earth is essentially, intentionally and constitutionally one," and to this they all agreed.

2. Like all of their principles, this one found abundant corroboration in the Scripture of the New Testament.

(a) It was the Master's desire and fervent prayer (John 17:21).

(b) Paul labored in his many letters to forestall divisions in the church (Rom. 12:16; 1 Cor. 1:10; 2 Cor. 13:11).

(c) Peter pleaded with "the elect" for this same thing (1 Pet. 3:8).

(d) Divine inspiration provided the very basis upon which the church should be united (Eph. 4:1-6).

3. The principle of Christian unity has been more widely accepted, and in that sense has been the greatest contribution of the movement to the Christian world of any of its principles. At the beginning of the nineteenth century Christian unity was not desired, and was even opposed by most of the churches, but today—thanks to more than a century of Restoration history—it is the universally accepted desire of all the churches.

III. The Spirit and Genius of the Restoration Movement May Be Seen from a Brief Consideration of Some of the Great Slogans Adopted.

A. *Prominent among these was the one given by Thomas Campbell,* "Where the Scriptures speak we speak, and where the Scriptures are silent we are silent."

1. A fearless proclamation of all the great teachings of the Bible was characteristic of the early preachers. To withhold and shun to "declare the whole counsel of God" was to fail to "speak where the Scriptures speak." It was this

Page 100

fearless stand that made of the pioneers great gospel preachers and gave impetus to their evangelistic program.

2. On the other hand, they were careful not to take a dogmatic stand for things not clearly revealed in the Word of God, or make them conditions of membership and fellowship in the church. Thus the cause was safeguarded from the error of adding to the Word in the writing of creeds, disciplines and articles of faith.

B. *Another slogan, closely related to the one above, was, "In essentials, unity; in opinions, liberty."*

1. In drawing a line of distinction between essentials and opinions, they made it clear that whatever was clearly taught in the Scriptures, "either by express command or approved precedent," was a matter of faith, and therefore essential, but whatever was not so taught belonged in the realm of human opinion, and all were left free to exercise their rights to private opinions.

2. This at once made it possible for the church to have a divine standard that was eternally fixed, and at the same time recognize a realm where "sanctified common sense" might adjust the program of the church to the ever changing and progressive conditions under which man lives.

C. *Another slogan much used was, "No book but the Bible; no creed but the Christ; no name but the divine name."*

In this slogan we can clearly see the catholicity of the plea of the Restoration movement. Discarding all other confessions of faith and creeds, they would stand upon the universally accepted ground of the Bible; discarding statements of belief concerning Christ and all the theological controversy surrounding the Christian system, they would accept Christ Himself as the supreme object of their faith, and, laying aside human names, they would adopt the name "Christian," which was universally accepted by all Christian bodies.

Thus from the great slogans of the movement may be seen the spirit and genius of it.

IV. While There Are Many Interrelated Principles of the Restoration Movement, We Believe They Can All Be Summed Up Under the Following Heads:

1. The Bible only as a rule of faith and practice.

2. The restoration of the church of the New Testament in all its essentials.

3. A proper distinction between the old and the new covenants.

4. The autonomy of the local church.

5. A recognition of Christ as the supreme authority in the church.

6. That "the church of Christ is essentially, intentionally and constitutionally one."

REVIEW

The answers to the questions used in this review are not given here, but Scripture references are given which should help the pupil to find the answers. With the exception of Lesson 1 of this review, the answers will not be exactly alike, for each pupil is left to express himself in his own way. The entire review lesson should be carefully studied by each pupil and the answers to all the questions fully determined before coming to class.

Bible Drill and Review of Lesson I

1. What are the divisions of the books of the Old Testament?
2. Name the books of the law.
3. Name the books of history.
4. Name the books of devotion.
5. Name the books of the minor prophets.
6. Name the books of the major prophets.
7. What are the divisions of the books of the New Testament?
8. Name the books of biography.
9. Name the book of history.
10. Name the books of special letters.
11. Name the books of general letters.
12. Name the book of prophecy.

Review of Lesson II

1. Give three reasons why the Bible is the most wonderful Book in the world (John 5:39; Eph. 6:17; 2 Tim. 3:15).

2. How should the Bible be read to be understood? (Acts 17:11; 2 Tim. 2:15.)

3. Give the "rule of three" for reading the Bible.

4. What kind of Bible helps should one have?

5. What should be our attitude of mind and heart in reading the Bible? (Ps. 1:1-6.)

Review of Lesson III

1. To what does Jesus liken the Word of God? (Matt. 13:18-23.)

2. Of what does Peter say we are born again? (1 Pet. 1:23.)

3. What part did the preaching of the Word play in New Testament conversions? (Acts 2:14-41; 7:54-60; 8:5-8, 12, 26-40; 10:34-48; 16:14, 15, 23-34.)

4. How have we been changed by the new birth? From what condition have we been saved? (Luke 15:3-32; Matt. 15:24.) In what way have our relationships been changed? (Col. 1:20, 21; Rom. 5:8-11.) In what way has our state been changed? (1 Cor. 15:22.)

5. In what way are we to separate ourselves from the world, and why?

Review of Lesson IV

1. Name at least eight ways in which the church is divine (Matt. 16:18; 1 Cor. 3:11; Col. 1:18; Isa. 62:2; Matt. 16:16; Eph. 5:30; John 16:13; 2 Tim. 3:16, 17).

2. In what ways have we underemphasized church attendance?

3. What is the great twofold work of the church?

Page 104

4. Give at least three instances of Christ's followers meeting together to worship (Luke 24:1-12, 33-35; Acts 1:12; 2:42; 20:7).

5. What is the fourfold program of worship that was practiced by the New Testament church? (Acts 2:42; 1 Cor. 11:26.)

Review of Lesson V

1. What ordinances of the Old Testament point to the atonement? (Ex. 12:1-28; 1 Cor. 5:7; Ex. 27:1-8; Heb. 9:11-28; Lev. 16:5, 20-22.)

2. Of what was the table of showbread typical? (Lev. 24:5-8; Ex. 25:29, 30; Matt. 26:25-29.)

3. How do we know the Lord's Supper is divinely given? (1 Cor. 11:23-25.)

4. How often should we observe the Lord's Supper? (1 Cor. 16:1, 2; Acts 20:7; 1 Cor. 11:20; Acts 2:42; Heb. 10:19-31.)

5. In what attitude of mind and heart should the Lord's Supper be observed? (1 Cor. 10:16; 11:26.)

6. Give a brief summary of this lesson.

Review of Lesson VI

1. Why is the Christian dispensation the dispensation of the Holy Spirit? (John 4:19-24; 14:15-17; 16:7, 8.)

2. Do we have the Holy Spirit today? (Acts 2:38, 39; 5:32; Rom. 5:5.)

3. Can the Holy Spirit be banished from our lives? (Eph. 4:30; Matt. 12:31, 32; 1 Thess. 5:19.)

4. What blessings will He work in our lives if we allow Him to remain? (Gal. 5:16, 22, 23.)

5. What relationship do we sustain to the Holy Spirit if we are truly Christian? (Rom. 8:1-4.)

Review of Lesson VII

1. How much emphasis did Jesus place upon prayer? (Matt. 14:13-33; 26:36-44; 27:46, 50; Mark 14:22, 23; Luke 3:21; 6:12, 13; John 17.)

2. Give at least three instances of the early church meeting to pray (Acts 1:12—2:1, 42; 12:1-13; 20:36; 21:3-5).

3. Why do we need to pray? (Matt. 26:41; Luke 18:1-8; Jas. 5:16.)

4. Will God hear sinners who pray to Him? (1 Pet. 3:12.)

5. Will He hear the prayers of the righteous? (Matt. 21:22; Jas. 5:13-18.)

6. What is essential to effective prayer? (Matt. 6:14, 15; Mark 11:24, 25; Luke 18:9-14; Rom. 8:26.)

Review of Lesson VIII

1. What two mistakes have we made in regard to the stewardship of our talents? (Matt. 25:14-30.)

2. What places of service does the New Testament provide? (Matt. 25:31-46; Acts 8:4; 14:23; 6:1-6; 1 Cor. 14:13-19; 2 Tim. 4:5; Col. 3:16.)

Review of Lesson IX

1. Why is the law of Christian giving a fundamental necessity? (Luke 6:38; Rom. 12:13; 1 Cor. 9:7-14.)

2. What teaching of the Scriptures leads us to think God does not require us to give up all we have? (Mark 10:29, 30; 1 Tim. 4:8; 5:8.)

3. Why are we to believe the Lord wants proportionate giving? (Matt. 22:21; 1 Cor. 16:1, 2.)

4. How should the Christian's giving compare with that of the Jew who gave the tithe? (Matt. 5:21, 22, 43, 44; Luke 11:42; Heb. 8:6; 11:40.)

Page 106